A User's Guide to Path Analysis

Moses E. Olobatuyi

UNIVERSITY PRESS OF AMERICA,® INC.
Lanham • Boulder • New York • Toronto • Oxford

Copyright © 2006 by
University Press of America,® Inc.
4501 Forbes Boulevard
Suite 200
Lanham, Maryland 20706
UPA Acquisitions Department (301) 459-3366

PO Box 317
Oxford
OX2 9RU, UK

Library of Congress Control Number: 2006922974
ISBN-13: 978-0-7618-3230-0 (clothbound : alk. paper)
ISBN-10: 0-7618-3230-0 (clothbound : alk. paper)
ISBN-13: 978-0-7618-3231-7 (paperback : alk. paper)
ISBN-10: 0-7618-3231-9 (paperback : alk. paper)

I dedicate this work to Olufunke, my wife, whose love, respect, and patience are always there; to Ayodeji, Abayomi, Olubunmi, Olayinka, and Odunola; and in loving memory of my parents, Abraham Olobatuyi Asamo and Elizabeth Aladeyemi Olobatuyi; my grandmother, Oguntomola; and my aunt, Remilekun, who named me "Akowe" (Writer).

Contents

Foreword

A User's Guide to Path Analysis presents a readable introduction for the beginning reader of path analysis and causal modeling. Moses Olobatuyi, a former student in my courses on statistics at Howard University, has taken seriously a departing challenge that I leave with all persons completing my courses: grow, and help others to grow, from what you have learned. Dr. Olobatuyi's book reflects his further study of several ideas associated with traditional applications of path analysis. These ideas are basic for understanding causal modeling as it has evolved over time.

Three aspects of the book make it important reading for the student new to path analysis. First, it bears repeating that the book is readable. This is not a small matter. Without special conduits, such as non-technical, historical, or easy-to-read discussions, by which to start the reading process of what can quickly become technically challenging reading, many will never begin the growth process of appreciating the role that statistical tools, like path analysis, can have for empowering them in their chosen work. Second, the reader will find a large segment of the relevant, especially early, literature on causal and scientific reasoning, identified and woven together in a discussion of the early issues and debates surrounding the introduction of path analytic procedures. Finally, distinct from its readability, *A User's Guide to Path Analysis* represents a useful first-step in a reader's maturational process to a more thorough understanding of today's expanding literature on causal and structural equation modeling. Understanding the basic terminology and processes presented in *A User's Guide to Path Analysis* can reduce the burden associated with more advanced reading, an exercise that this book can motivate.

Ron Carmichael Manuel, Ph.D.
Department of Sociology & Anthropology
Howard University

Preface

WHAT IS THE PURPOSE OF THIS BOOK?

This book serves many purposes through its contributions to scholarship in different ways. It facilitates conceptual understanding of path analysis by limiting the technical nature of the discussion of those concepts, and instead focusing on their practical applications. It provides graduate students taking advanced statistics and their teachers as well as researchers with skills needed in applying path analysis in their research through a step-by-step approach. It also provides students, teachers and researchers with the skills necessary to interpret research articles that have employed path analysis. It further provides an easy to read textbook that prepares or guides graduate students, teachers and researchers to apply path analysis to the processing and interpretation of their own data. Its coverage of the sequence of activities in path analysis from its historical background to the interpretation and presentation of results adds to our knowledge of the technique. As a result, the statistical procedure has been taken care of by presenting it in a conceptual context that explains why the procedure was developed and when and how it should be used.

WHO IS THE INTENDED AUDIENCE?

The book is written for graduate students in the social sciences (Economics, Political Science, Psychology, Sociology) who are taking advanced statistics as part of their degree requirements. At a broader level, the book may be useful as both a reference material and a textbook for graduate courses. The book is also intended for a broader audience of faculty, professionals and researchers in many disciplines and fields such as criminal justice, marketing, sociology, education, health professions, and social work.

HOW IS THIS BOOK ORGANIZED?

The book is structured to cover the sequence of activities that should be covered in applying path analysis. The introductory chapter contains basic information in path analysis, including its historical development, controversies and conditions for causality, uses, issues, contributions and limitations. Chapter 2 presents the definitions of basic terms and concepts usually used in path analysis, with graphical illustrations. Chapter 3 focuses on construction of a causal diagram with emphasis on variable positioning, path symbols, error terms, missing arrows, and feedback loops. Chapter 4 discusses the assumptions underlying path analysis, including the rationale, tests for possible violations, effects of violations, and justification for using path analysis despite assumption violations. Chapter 5, "Causal Model Estimation," considers the two major problems in path analysis: estimation of path coefficients and decomposition of correlations into causal parameters in which two methods of decomposition—the numeric or algebraic method and the path tracing method—are discussed with illustrations. In Chapter 6, practical research questions needed in interpreting a path model are considered. One research question centers on assessing the adequacy of the model. The other questions are about assessing the specific aspects of the model. Chapter 7 concludes the exercise with six principles researchers should follow in reading a path diagram, how to interpret the results generated by computer, information the researcher should include in writing or interpreting his or her findings, and SPSS computer program for path analysis.

WHAT IS UNIQUE ABOUT THIS BOOK?

Compared with other books on path analysis, this book has the following unique features. It is not technically or mathematically oriented like other textbooks on path analysis. This unique feature has the potential of making it appealing to students in the social and behavioral sciences, education and epidemiology, who are not majoring in statistics and research methodology. The book covers a sequence of activities needed in understanding and using path analysis from its historical background to the interpretation and presentation of results and how to use the SPSS program. Such a sequence of activities has hardly been put together in any of the mainstream textbooks on path analysis.

Unlike other textbooks, in which the definition of terms is in the glossary section, Chapter 2 of the book is devoted to definition of terms and concepts that students, teachers and researchers frequently use in path analysis. As a result, the chapter offers a language lesson with graphical illustrations to help readers to understand subsequent chapters. The chapter on assumptions, Chapter 4, presents statements of assumptions, rationales for the assumptions, testing for violations, effects of violations, and justification for using path analysis when assumptions are violated. These are rarely put together in other textbooks. Each chapter contains an extensive list of references for further reading to help the reader. Because of these unique features, including its step-by-step teaching approach, the book fulfills its purpose as a handbook on path analysis.

Moses E. Olobatuyi
Baltimore, Maryland
October 2004.

Acknowledgments

I wish to thank Drs. Catherine Zimmer of the Department of Sociology and Anthropology, North Carolina State University; Ron C. Manuel of the Department of Sociology and Anthropology, Howard University; and Samuel C. Ndubuisi, Health Statistician, HIV Aids-Bureau, U.S. Department of Health and Human Services, Rockville, Maryland for their comments and suggestions through their gracious review of the manuscript.

I also want to thank Drs. Frederick C. Jones of the Department of English, Saint Augustine's College; Marc E. Waddell of the Department of English, Morris College; Joshua O. Olowe of the Department of English, Obafemi University, Nigeria for their editorial assistance and suggestions and Dr. Lal Shimpi of the Division of Business, Saint Augustine's College for his assistance in computer diagramming and imaging.

Chapter One

Introduction

The occurrence of any event is usually attributed to different causes in different societies. That is, different societies try to answer questions about why an event occurred. Such "Why Questions" are usually answered based on the experiences, traditions and level of development, religious beliefs, and level of education of the members of the particular society.

In traditional societies, the death of an infant or an incurable disease may be attributed to witchcraft or sorcery. The religiously inclined may see it as an act of God or the penalty for sins, but a medical doctor would explain it as occurring due to lack of medical care or an unhygienic lifestyle. For instance, some centuries ago, according to a legend, a serious tornado destroyed many houses, farms and livestock in a town, Ikere- Ekiti, in Nigeria. Being a very religious society, the towns-people attributed the cause of such a deadly event to the wrath of their god, *Olosunta*, whom they believed was angry with them for their failure to perform the religious sacrifice of a cow to appease the god. Here, the Ikere people, because of their religious inclination, went for esoteric measures to solve a practical problem. But in modern societies of today, the practice is to look for practical causes to solve mundane problems. Natural disasters like floods, tornadoes, hurricanes, which were attributed to the wrath of some gods many centuries ago, are now being explained by meteorologists as climatic conditions.

In recent years, social scientists in the United States (Blau and Duncan 1972) have been faced with the question of whether children's occupation is causally related to their parents' education. In fact, people in different societies at different stages of development have been wrestling with the "Why Questions" (Causation) for many years before the birth of modern science and philosophy. This book will explore the concept of causation and discuss

1

its relationship to path analysis with particular emphasis on the guidelines for users of path analysis.

THE HISTORICAL DEVELOPMENT OF PATH ANALYSIS

The notion of causation has been one of the most dominant analytic concerns in the history of science. Also the nature of causation has led to serious debates among philosophers and scientists for many years. For a detailed historical review of the philosophical thinking about causality, see Bunge (1959); Wallace (1972, and 1974). In this section, the historical development of causation discussed by Bagozzi (1980); Sobel (1995); Cook and Campbell (1979); and Berk (1988) is summarized.

In the early stage of the development of causation, Aristotle's (1930) attempt to answer the "Why Questions" provided probably the first detailed analysis of "cause," which he grouped into four types: The definable cause, which is roughly the shape, pattern, nature or structure of a thing functioning as a cause; the antecedent cause, which necessitates a consequence referred to as "that out of which (*ex hou*), as a constituent, something is generated" (Wallace 1972: 14); the efficient cause, which started the process referred to as the source of change or its cessation as exemplified in the actions of a social actor or an external physical force; and the final cause, which refers to the purpose or end for which a thing is done. He explained further that the goal of a scientific explanation is knowledge, which, in turn, depends fundamentally on the nature of causality.

During the middle ages, scholars in European institutions such as Oxford University, The University of Paris, and the University of Padua were concerned with causal explanations they thought were central to their empirical research. One of the scholars during that time was Galileo, who in 1638 tried to find the true causes, "*Verae Causae*," of any phenomena. He concluded that the true causes of the occurrence of any event consisted of both the necessary and sufficient conditions. Unlike Aristotle's theorem, which emphasized the importance of the nature of a cause in producing an effect, Galileo's conclusion presented an early analysis of the logic and empirical requirement concerning the cause and effect relationship. Thus, a cause is always followed by an effect and when that cause is removed, the effect will definitely disappear. This conclusion was in conformity with the empiricist and positivist conceptions of causality and makes him one of the first to suggest that causal relations entail contiguity and constant conjunction between cause and effect.

While the philosophical consideration of causality began with Aristotle's physics, it was David Hume's analysis of causation (1978, 1988, 1988) that provided a convenient starting point for the current ferment about causal inference (Sobel 1995; Berk 1988). David Hume identified three conditions for inferring causal relations as contiguity between the presumed cause and effect; temporal priority or precedence, in that cause had to precede the effect in time; and constant conjunction, in that the cause had to be present whenever the effect was obtained. He did not accept that things could be causes, because changes in events or processes are causes. According to him, the idea of a cause producing an effect is an illusion, a psychological phenomenon, and a subjective feeling in the mind of the observer inferred from an observed association between events. For instance, one can only observe the sequence in which one billiard ball hits a second and the second ball falls into the pocket, but one cannot "prove" that the first ball "caused" the second to fall into the pocket. According to Berk (1988:156), "To this day, there is no effective rebuttal. Causal statements are always inferential statements." Hume's analysis has been criticized extensively. For detailed review of the criticism, see Sobel (1995:5-6). Immanuel Kant (1961) disagrees with Hume's idea that the necessity between cause and effect is psychological. He states that a connection between cause and effect involves "a form of non-logical, non-empirical necessity and that this necessity is a pre-rational pattern imposed by the mind."

Despite Hume's enormous contributions to causal inference, current empirical works of sociology rest far more on methods proposed by John Stuart Mill (1973). Mill held that causal inference depends on three factors: the cause has to precede the effect in time; the cause and effect have to be related; and other explanations of the cause-effect relationship have to be eliminated. Through these criteria, Mill made great methodological contributions to the notion of causation and derived the procedures for discovering and demonstrating the standards for causal relationship in modern experimental research. Based on the three factors, he proposed a set of five canons for causal inferences: the method of agreement, the method of difference, the method of concomitant variation, the joint method of agreement and difference, and the method of residues. In fact, the first three canons for causal inferences are related to his third factor of causal inference. These provide the basis for the scientific investigation of causal laws, especially those commonly used in sociology. For a good summary of Mill's approach, see Cohen and Nagel (1934:250).

During the 20th century, inquiry into the concept of causation nearly came to a stand still because some philosophers actually questioned whether causation exists at all. Others, like Bertrand Russell (1912-1913), relegated it to the domain of myth not worthy of serious investigation despite other debates on different aspects of causation among philosophers and scientists reported by Sobel (1995:7-31); Bagozzi (1980:11-30); Cook and Campbell (1979:20-36); and Maxim (1999:chapter 3). But how did the concept of causation make its way into the social sciences? For many years, sociologists have used the classical statistical methods such as regressions to analyze varieties of sociological data. With these methods, they were only able to predict the change of one variable as result of a change in another, but they could not incorporate statistical results into social theory, nor were they able to evaluate or reformulate sociological theory. Such a gap between our scientific theory and empirical research, and the suggestions that causal modeling as a technique can improve our ability to make causal inferences from field study data stimulated the discussion or discovery of linear causal models or path analysis (Land 1969; Blalock 1968a; Bentler 1980; Heise 1975; Kenny 1979). Causal modeling is also referred to as path analysis.

Path analysis is the statistical technique used to examine causal relationships between two or more variables. It is based upon a linear equation system and was first developed by Sewall Wright, a geneticist, in the 1920s for use in the phylogenetic studies he published in many essays in 1921, 1934, 1954,1960. He did not see the technique as a method to discover causes but as a method applied to a causal model formulated by the researcher on the basis of knowledge and theoretical consideration. He developed a number of concepts important to the present day use of path analysis, including, for example, path coefficients, and the use of multiplications rule to determine the indirect effects of one variable upon another. Path analysis was adopted by the social sciences in the 1960s and has been used with increasing frequency in the ecological literature since the 1970s. Blalock (1964) introduced this statistical breakthrough in agriculture into social sciences through his book entitled "Causal Inferences in Non Experimental Research." In 1968, he published essays dealing with problems in the methodology of causal model and in 1982 laid emphasis on the importance of theoretical assumptions in causal models. In the last few decades, techniques for causal inference from non-experimental data have emerged as a dominant method within sociology, economics, and political science under such names as "causal models," "path analysis," and "structural equation models." In this work, the term "path analysis" will be used. Other social scientists followed the lead of Blalock. In his 1965 essay entitled "A Method of Linear Causal Analysis: Dependence Analysis," Boudon presented a thorough discussion of causal models and pointed out that the Simon-Blalock model is a weak form of path analysis because it did not contain convincing empirical illustration. Boudon also published an essay in 1968 entitled "A new look on correlation analysis," in which he reviewed his earlier result and generalized the analysis to a nonlinear structural equation.

The relationship between structural equation and path analysis was the contribution of Duncan. In 1966, he showed such a relationship and also gave many examples of the utility of path analysis in doing sociological research, and in 1975 he covered all aspects of structural equations in path models. The methodological principles and logic to follow in using path models were laid down in Land's (1969) essay entitled "Principles of Path Analysis," and Heise (1969) points out the basic assumptions or conditions that must be met in order to use path analysis and causal inference procedures. In 1975, Heise also gave a comprehensive treatment of causal modeling covering all aspects of path analysis with adequate discussion of current issues of the technique.

Through the contributions of these scholars and others, the technique has gained strong currency among sociologists since 1920 as a major analytic tool that provides a procedure for incorporating statistical results into social theory. Even Coser (1975) criticized many sociological journal editors for refusing to accept contributions not using regression and path analysis.

THE CONTROVERSY OVER CAUSATION

The concept of causation has stirred a great deal of controversy among philosophers and scientists but much of the debates stems from David Hume's analysis of causation explained earlier in the chapter (For more details see Blalock 1964, 1971; Braithwaite 1953; Cook and Campbell 1979; Feigl and Brodbeck 1953; Hanson 1958, 1971; Scriven 1971, 1975; and Simon 1957, 1968). Also noted earlier, even Bertrand Russell (1912-1913:180) and Kerlinger (1973:393) relegated it to the domain of myth, not worthy of scientific investigation. It is not the purpose of the present author to take any side of the debate but to draw attention to the fact that causal thinking still plays a significant role in many scientific studies. In the work of scientists, even among those who strongly opposed the use of the term "causation," terms that imply causal thinking are commonly used. This is well noted by some scholars: Lerner (1965) reported that a colloquium of philosophers of science concluded that the idea of causal thinking has gained wide currency among them, and Suppes (1970:5-6) claimed that his review of literature shows that physicists, commonly and widely used causality and cause in their advanced work. Causality is at the center of inquiry in sociology, psychology, economics, marketing, political science and other areas in the behavioral sciences (Blalock 1971, 1974; Goldberger and Duncan 1973; McClelland 1975; Brodbeck 1963:2). It is not only the philosophers and scientists that think in causal terms, it is human nature to think in causal terms. For example, Sobel (1995) states that Young (1978) expresses that human beings have the propensity to think in causal terms and Einhorn and Hogarth (1986) and White and Hogarth (1990) have shown in their studies how human beings make judgments about causation in their daily lives.

In sum, even though on philosophical grounds, scientists, qua scientists, may have reservations about the term causation, the method and practice continues to play a significant role in their scientific research (Nagel 1965; Pedhazur 1982) and have found working with causal hypothesis to be a very productive way of doing science (Blalock, 1964:6).

CONDITIONS FOR CAUSALITY

A causal relation never occurs in isolation. Hume (1739) argues that it is not easy to show a material or ontological relationship between cause and effect, and Bridgman (1927) notes that it is not simple to say that event "A" is connected with event "B" without including the whole background of the system in which the events occur in the concept. In spite of this philosophical debate, the concept of causation is strongly ingrained in science and in our daily thinking. There is no other choice than to work with this concept while being very careful in our definition of cause. As social scientists, we can say that variable X causes variable Y if the following conditions are present (Babbie 2004; Seltiz et al. 1959; Bailey 1994; Elifson et al. 1998): (a) There must be co-variation or association between the two variables. That is, the two variables should systematically vary with each other; when a change in X occurs a change in Y must also occur. Such change could be positive or negative; (b) there must be time order, in that a cause must precede the effects. For causality to occur, the change in X must precede in time the change in Y. In a nontechnical form, the cause must occur before the effect. For instance, there is a causal relationship between a dead man and a gunshot only if the man died after he was shot; and (c) non spuriousness: association between two variables, X and Y, should not be explained by a third variable, Z. That is, the relationship between X and Y must not arise from another common causal factor, Z, as shown thus:

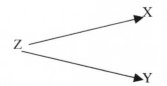

Figure 1.1.   Spurious Associations

No spurious relationship exists between X and Y if the diagram is X→Y because the relationship between the two variables is not due to a common causal factor.

One can also talk about causality in terms of necessary and sufficient conditions (Mackie 1965, 1974; Von Wright 1971, 1974; Cook and Campbell 1979; Bailey 1994) in that X is necessary for the existence of Y if Y never occurs unless X occurs. X is sufficient for the existence of Y if Y occurs every time that X occurs. Decasse (1951) proposed three combinations of necessary and sufficient conditions: (a) X is a necessary but not a sufficient condition for the existence of Y when X must occur before Y can occur, but X alone is not enough to cause the occurrence of Y. Other factors must occur in addition to X before Y can occur. That is, X is a partial cause of Y. It combines with other factors to cause Y to occur; (b) X is a sufficient but not a necessary condition to cause Y to occur. There are many alternative factors each of which is sufficient to cause Y to occur. X is not a partial but an alternative factor among other factors that can cause Y to occur; (c) X is both a necessary and a sufficient condition for the existence of Y. Here Y will never exist unless X occurs and will always occur when X occurs. That is, X is the only and complete cause of Y. There are no other alternative causes.

THE USES OF PATH ANALYSIS

Path analysis can be used in many ways by researchers in different disciplines. A political scientist may use it to determine whether a Congress representative's voting behavior is caused by his/her personal beliefs and attitude or his/her expectations of constituent attitudes, or how the President signs a bill is due to his personal belief and attitude or expectation of his political party. A sociologist may want to determine whether an adolescent's vocational aspirations are caused by his/her level of education, parent's career achievements, or by socio-economic environment and peers' expectation, or whether children's education is caused by parent's education and occupation. A criminologist may want to examine whether juvenile delinquency is causally related to a broken home and the lack of parental supervision. It is a good technique for an economist to determine whether unemployment is causally related to wage rates, government expenditure and other variables. An educator may use it to examine whether scores on achievement tests are causally related to ethnicity, sex, level of education and the environment. A behavioral geneticist may try to determine the causal relationship between genotypic values, environmental values and phenotypic values. An epidemiologist may use path analysis to determine whether hypertension is causally related to race or class. A psychologist may argue that people react to stimuli by forming cognitive or affective judgments, and that subsequent behavior is stimulated by these judgments:

Stimulus Condition → Variables That Express Thought Elements → Behavior. Social workers may use path analysis to determine whether depressed persons in support groups fare better than those in antidepressant drug treatment; whether one person has an effect on others' behavior; whether reality orientation, reminiscence groups, or validation therapy is most effective with disoriented aged persons; and whether young people take better precautions against AIDS if they are exposed to peer counseling or to an informational program conducted by their teachers. The industrial sales marketing researcher may apply path analysis to study the effects of performance on job satisfaction or the influence of role ambiguity and achievement motivation on job outcomes.

PRACTICAL ISSUES IN PATH ANALYSIS

Not only has the notion of causation generated much controversy among philosophers and scientists, like other statistical techniques, its application has also led to some debates among social scientists and researchers. These issues discussed by Asher (1976); Bagozzi (1980); Ellis (1994); and Maxim (1999) center on the following core areas of its application as summarized below.

Interpretation of path coefficients (pij) has raised some discussions among researchers. Some have argued that path coefficients should be interpreted as measuring the fraction of the standard deviation of the dependent variable explained by the independent variable, but others have interpreted it as the proportion of the variance in the dependent variable directly accounted for by the independent variable in question (See Land 1969; Duncan 1970 for a detailed review).

The debate on how to solve over-identification problems in recursive models led to the following suggestions: minimization of sum of squares for obtaining the path estimates that utilize the information provided by all equations (Bourdon 1968); using ordinary least squares because it has smaller sampling variability (Goldberger 1970); using maximum likelihood estimator, which is equivalent to the ordinary least square estimates (Land 1973); and deleting some paths and then retesting the model until the model is identified (Wonnacott and Wonnacott 1970; Uslane 1976).

The type of research in which to use standardized (β) as opposed to un-standardized (b) coefficients was another issue (Blalock 1967; Forbes and Turfte

1968; Turkey 1954; Turner and Steven 1959; and Wright 1960). Among a variety of suggestions, the following view by Blalock was the most acceptable: Standardized coefficients (β) should be used only when researchers desire to generalize to a specific population or compare the relative importance of independent variables on the same dependent variable within a population and can lead to false inferences when used to make comparison across populations or samples; and un-standardized coefficients (b) should be used for making comparison across populations to determine whether the underlying causal processes are similar. In fact, Schoenberg (1972) shows the conditions when un-standardized coefficients may be inappropriate. For example, Specht and Warren (1975) used un-standardized coefficients for comparing causal models and individual parameters across population.

The types of research in which cause and effect relationships can be inferred remain a serious issue among researchers. The question is, "Is experimentation a necessary condition for science (causality)?" Holland (1986) argues that it is through experimentation that any degree of causality can be imputed, and Gravetter and Wallnau (2004) assert that the goal of experiment is to establish a cause and effect relationship through manipulation of variables and control over the research situation. Some researchers question the widespread use of causal analysis in the social sciences (sociology, political science, and economics) to make causal inferences in non-experimental research (Gordon 1967; Coser 1975;Wilson and Hernstein 1985:156) because non-experimental research methods do not set out, nor can they test, any causal relationship between variables (Salkind 2003) and all extraneous variables that might confound such relationships cannot be statistically controlled (Frankfort-Nachmias and Nachmias 1992:417). Others argue that non-experimental research could be used to infer cause and effect relationship in the social sciences to explain social phenomena. In fact, Nagel (1961:452-453) asserts that many sciences always contribute to the advancement of generalized knowledge despite their limited opportunities for instituting controlled experiments, and what is needed is controlled investigation because science can progress even when it meets only the weak assumptions of causality.

How to solve the problem of sizable standard error of the estimated regression coefficients caused by a high level of collinearity is another issue in path analysis. Some investigators have argued that because multicollinearity is due to instability of sample estimates researchers should not worry about the problem when they are working with the entire population. Others have argued that using the entire population rather than the sample may not solve the problem because multicollinearity is more likely to be a problem with aggregate data (data collected for groups and the characteristics of individual respondents are no longer identifiable) than with survey data (data collected on individuals). This is because, in aggregating observations, the random measurement error component of the score is likely to be cancelled, whereas in survey data, random measurement error is ever present. The presence of random error reduces correlation coefficients, thereby making the problem of collinearity less likely. Furthermore, large sample sizes can reduce the impact of collinearity in survey data than in aggregate data. Therefore, the problem is the type of data rather than the size of the sample (For more detail, see Deegan 1972; Blalock 1963; Farrar and Glauber 1967).

The issue of explanation across levels of analysis that arises when researchers include both social and psychological variables in their theories to explain cause and effect relationship is another dilemma for researchers. Explanation across levels of analysis can enrich our theories, enhance our predictions, and aid social planners in making decisions. But the possibility of spurious relationships and false inferences cannot be ignored. Therefore, researchers must use good logic and sound theory to specify the linkages of association of concepts from different levels of social phenomena because it is usually impossible to experimentally manipulate variables to ascertain causality.

How to solve the effects of measurement error led to the following suggestions: using measures of the same variables from the same units at multiple points in time, such as panel data (Heise 1971, Wiley and Wiley 1971); using instrumental variable or multiple indicators of the same variable (Heise 1975; Costner 1971); and that such consequences can be assessed by knowing the true scores of the variable (Siegel and Hodge 1968). For more details, see Land (1970); Hauser and Goldberger (1971); Werts, Joreskog and Linn (1973); Wiley (1973); Blalock et al.(1970); and Asher (1974).

Solutions to sampling errors remain a controversial issue. When there is a sample error, pxy will not equal rxy. That is, the correlation in the sample is not equal to the correlation in the population. This problem can be solved by increasing the sample size and then apply the Central Limit Theorem which states that the greater the samples, the less will the error be no matter the shape of the population distribution. That is, the sampling distribution of x approaches the shape of the normal curve as sample size increases even when the samples are drawn from populations that are known to be non-normal.

How to estimate models with correlated error terms across indicators of separate theoretical variables is another issue. That is, two exogenous variables (X_1, X_2) influence a theoretical variable (X_3) that in turn is reciprocally related to another theoretical variable, X_4. In such a model, the error terms for X_3 and X_4 will correlate as diagramed thus:

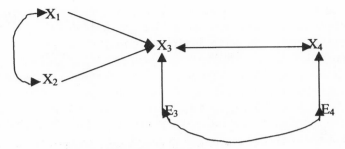

Figure 1.2. Correlated Error Terms

When error terms are correlated, researchers should employ generalized least squares (GLS) or Two-stage Least Squares, instead of ordinary least squares, to estimate path coefficients (James and Singh 1978).

The serious effects of using ordinal data when interval data are not available have led to different conclusions. Wilson (1971) and others argued that such violation will lead to inconclusive results and that any attempt to transform such data as a solution may reverse the result. Others have rejected such a conclusion, and asserted that using ordinal instead of interval level measurement should not be a serious problem in that it allows researchers to use more powerful and sophisticated statistical techniques like Monte Carlo, but we should be careful not to willingly violate such an assumption (Bohrnstedt and Carter 1971; Labovitz 1967, 1970; Mayer 1970, 1971; and Asher 1976).

THE CONTRIBUTIONS AND
LIMITATIONS OF PATH ANALYSIS

As a statistical technique, path analysis has contributed immensely to the analysis and interpretation of social data.

Path analysis presents the statement of an explicit theory about relationships between variables rather than simply testing a set of data for any linear relationship. It also produces a clear and explicit result of the strength of the mathematical relationships contained within.

Regression is merely an analysis of correlating mathematical relationships performed in a very specific way. But path analysis is a much more specific form of analysis that looks explicitly at cause. It is used in studying the properties of systems more complicated than those of a straight regression setup. So path analysis is superior to ordinary regression analysis because it allows us to examine the causal processes underlying the observed relationship and to estimate the relative importance of alternative paths of influence.

By using path analysis, researchers are able to simultaneously assess various types of relations among variables and rigorously examine and compare similarities among and differences between groups of study.

By computing the path coefficients, we are able to measure the magnitude of change in each dependent variable predicted by the independent variable in the model. Examining the path coefficient of the residual path analysis provides a convenient and logical calculation and interpretation of the coefficients of alienation (residual) as the percentage of variance in each dependent variable due to outside variables not included in the model.

Path analysis also enables us to measure the direct and indirect effects that one variable has upon another. Through this, we can compare the magnitude of the direct and indirect effects, which would identify the operative causal mechanism. It also provides another methodological advantage in that researchers can use multiple measures as both independent and dependent variables.

The decomposition of the path coefficients in path analysis, into its component parts—direct effects, indirect effects, unanalyzed correlation and spurious effects—provides a general procedure for exploring these effects of a determining variable on a dependent variable in a multivariate model and thereby provides us an interpretation of these effects. This is a better way to understand the correlations that we observe in terms of how much is due to direct effects, indirect effects and third variables.

Path analysis depicts a mathematical model that is hypothesized to explain the correlations among variables. The technique was originally developed by Sewall Wright to solve intricate genetic problems. It has since been adopted by virtually all the behavioral sciences and applied to a large number of non-genetic research questions. This statistical technique is appropriate for testing some of the complicated sociological models that have been advanced and bridging the gap between our scientific theory and empirical research. For detailed review, see Land (1969); Burr et al. (1979a, 1979b); Wright (1931); Duncan (1966); and Dilalla (2000).

Despite these contributions, path analysis is not without some limitations. The language with which causal modeling is normally discussed; such as associational or temporal relations, is a problem to users. Some readers fail to understand that correlation does not imply causality. Some users of path analysis seem to believe that confirmation of a causal model implies proof, or that the model has been validated.

Causal models are often applied to data sets where information was collected for independent, intervening, and dependent variables in a single cross-sectional study from a single - wave field study or panel study data from a two - wave study, despite the fact that, in such cases, evidence of intervening variables must be gathered coincidentally with evidence for independent or dependent variables.

Due to the fact that very strict assumptions are required in path analysis, the variables we use in the social sciences are mostly at the nominal or ordinal level of measurement. As a result assumptions of normality, interval level scale and linearity are sometimes violated.

Investigators and methodologists do not take the implicit notion of causation seriously because they do not distinguish between variables that are causes and other variables that are concomitant (Sobel 1995, Kenny 1979:52). Whether a variable is designated the cause or effect depends on its usage. For example, children's education could be an endogenous variable if we wished to predict it from their father's education. Or a father's education could be an endogenous variable if we wish to predict it from his children's education. The point is that a variable must be placed into a framework or research situation before it can be designated as either exogenous or endogenous.

Results could be easily misinterpreted when researchers are anxious to "prove" the validity of a model or assess causality between variables when research design does not allow for such conclusion and incorrectly reported if user does not read and input correctly or read the output (including error messages) accurately (Dilalla 2000).

Investigators attempt to consider direct effects of alleged causes, even when it is clear that one or more intervening variables [the concept of an intervening variable is not even defined in the usual literature, as pointed out in Sobel (1990)] cannot be held constant.

The results of path analysis depend on whether causation is instantaneous or whether the cause is temporally prior to the effect. Researchers view temporal priority as one of the conditions in path analysis, but this is not reflected in their interpretation of the result, nor in the definition of the effects. Sobel (1990) explains how the mathematical results may hinge on explicit assumptions about such matters.

Investigators often treat simultaneity in path models as meaning that cause and effect simultaneously cause each other (Cox 1992). For additional criticism of causal modeling approach, see Holland (1988) and Sobel (1990).

Path analysis is most likely to be useful when we already have a clear hypothesis to test, or a small number of hypotheses all of which can be represented within a single path diagram. It has little use at the exploratory stage of research or in situations where "feedback" loops are included in our hypotheses: there must be a steady causal progression across (or down) a path diagram.

Path analysis can evaluate causal hypotheses, and in some (restricted) situations can test between two or more causal hypotheses, but it cannot establish the direction of causality.

Possible relations among exogenous variables are sometimes ignored when total effects of exogenous variables are computed. For example, in Figure 7.1, which includes a father's education and a mother's education, the total effect of a father's education on his children's education when reported may ignore the fact that a mother's education depends on and is temporally subsequent to a father's education. This shows that while both variables may be exogenous in the statistical sense with respect to children's education, it is difficult to argue that a father's education is determined outside the model.

All relationships in the path diagram must be capable of being tested by straightforward multiple regression. The intervening variables all have to serve as dependent variables in multiple regression analyses. Therefore each of them must be capable of being treated as being on an interval scale. Nominal measurement, or ordinal measurement with few categories (including dichotomies), will make path analysis impossible.

OVERVIEW OF SPECIFIC CHAPTERS

Applying path analysis can be viewed as a sequence of activities. This introductory chapter contains basic information in path analysis that includes its historical development, controversies and conditions for causality, uses, issues, contributions and limitations. The following chapters cover activities ranging from definition of basic terms and concepts to information for interpretation of results. In Chapter 2, basic terms and concepts usually used in path analysis are defined. Chapter 3 focuses on how to construct a causal diagram with emphasis on variable positioning, path symbols, error terms, missing arrows, and feedback loops. Chapter 4 discusses the assumptions underlying path analysis. Eleven assumptions are considered, each of which is treated under the following subheadings: (i) Explicit statement of the assumption; (ii) The rationale for the assumption: (iii) How to test the assumption for possible violations; and (iv) Justification for using path analysis despite assumption violations. Chapter 5, "Causal Model Estimation" considers the two major problems in path analysis. One is on estimation of path coefficients. The other is on decomposition of correlations into causal parameters in which two methods of decomposition, the numeric or algebraic method and the path tracing method, are discussed with illustrations. In Chapter 6, practical research questions needed in interpreting a path model are considered. One research question centers on assessing the adequacy of the model. The other questions are about assessing the specific aspects of the model. Chapter 7 concludes the activities with six principles researchers should follow in reading a path diagram, how to interpret the results generated by computer, information the researcher should include in writing or reporting his or her findings, and the SPSS computer program for path analysis.

REFERENCES

Asher, Herbert B. 1974. "Some Consequences of Measurement Error in Survey Data." *American Journal of Political Science* 18 (May): 469-485.
———. 1976. *Causal Modeling*. Beverly Hills: Sage Publications.
Aristotle. [350 B.C.E.] 1930. *The Works of Aristotle In Physica*, translated by R. P. Hardie and R. K. Gaye, Vol. 2. London: Oxford.
Babbie, Earl. 2004. *The Practice of Social Research*. Belmount, California: Wadsworth Publishing Company.
Bagozzi, Richard P. 1980. *Causal Models in Marketing*. New York: John Wiley & Sons.
Bailey, Kenneth D. 1994. *Methods of Social Research*. New York: The Free Press.
Bentler, P. M. 1980. "Multivariate Analysis with Latent Variables: Causal Modeling." *Annual Review of Psychology* 31:419-436.
Berk, Richard A. 1988. "Causal Inferences for Sociological Data." Pp. 155-172 in *Handbook of Sociology* edited by Neil J. Smelser. Newbury Park, CA: Sages.
Blalock, H. M.1963. "Correlated Independent Variables: The Problem of Multicollinearity." *American Journal of Sociology* 42:233-237.
———.1964. *Causal Inferences in Non-experimental Research*. Chapel Hill: University of North Carolina.
———. 1967. "Causal Inference, Closed Population, and Measures of Association." *American Political Science Review* 61(March): 130–136.
———. 1968a. "The Measurement Problem: A Gap Between the Language of Theory and Research." Pp. 5-27 in *Methodology in Social Research*, edited by H. M. Blalock and A. B. Blalock. New York: McGraw Hill.
———. 1968b. "Theory Building and Causal Inferences." Pp. 155- 198 in *Methodology in Social Research*, edited by H. M. Blalock and A. B. Blalock. New York: McGraw Hill.
———. 1971. "Causal Models Involving Unmeasured Variables in Stimulus Response Situations." Pp.335-367 in *Causal Models in the Social Sciences*, edited by H. M. Blalock, Jr. Chicago: Aldine- Atherton.
———. 1974. *Measurement in the Social Sciences: Theories and Strategies*. Chicago: Aldine Atherton.
———. 1982. *Conceptualization and Measurement in Social Sciences*. Beverly Hill: Sage Publications.
Blalock, H. M., C. S. Wells, and L. F. Carter. 1970. "Statistical Estimation with Random Measurement Error." Pp.75-103 in *Sociological Methodology*, edited by E. F. Borgatta and G.W. Bohrnstedt. San Francisco: Jossey Bass.

Blau, Peter M. and Otis Dudley Duncan. 1972. *The American Occupational Structure*. New York: John Wiley.

Bohrnstedt, G. W. and T. M.Carter. 1971. "Robustness in Regression Analysis." Pp.118-146 in *Sociological Methodology*, edited by H. L. Costner. San Francisco: Jossey-Bass.

Braithwaite, R. B.1953. *Scientific Explanation*. Cambridge: Cambridge University Press.

Bridgman, P. W. 1927. *The Logic of Modern Physics*. New York: Macmillian.

Brodbeck, May. 1963. "Logic and Scientific Methods in Research on Teaching." Pp.44-93 in *Handbook of Research on Teaching*, edited by N. J. Gage. Skokie, lll: Rand McNally.

Boudon, R. 1965. "A Method of Linear Causal Analysis: Dependence Analysis." *American Sociological Review* 30 (June): 365-374.

———. 1968. "A New Look at Correlation Analysis." Pp. 199-235 in *Methodology in Social Research*, edited by H. M. Blalock and A. B. Blalock. New York: McGraw Hill.

Bunge, M. 1959. *Causality*. Cambridge Mass: Harvard University Press.

Burr, W. R., R. Hill, F I. Nye, and I. L. Reiss. 1979a. *Contemporary Theories About the Family*. (Vol.1). New York: The Free Press.

———. 1979b. *Contemporary Theories About the Family*. (Vol.2). New York: The Free Press.

Cohen, Morris R. and Ernest Nagel. 1934. An Introduction to Logic and Scientific Method. New York: Harcourt Brace.

Cook, Thomas D. and Donald T. Campbell. 1979. *Quasi-Experimentation: Design and Analysis Issues for Field Settings*. Hopewell, N. J.: Houghton Mifflin Co.

———. 1979. *Quasi-Experimentation: Design and Analysis Issues for Field Settings*. Stokie, lll: Rand McNally.

Coser, Lewis A. 1975. "Presidential Address: Two Methods in Search of a Substance." *American Sociological Review* Vol. 40, No. 6 (December): 691-700.

Costnner, H. L.1971. "Theory, Deduction, and Rules of Correspondence." Pp. 299-326. in *Causal Models in the Social Sciences*, edited by H. M. Blalock. Chicago: Aldine-Atherton.

Cox, D. R. 1992. "Causality: Some Statistical Aspects." *Journal of the Royal Statistical Society* Ser. A, 155:291-301.

Deegan, J. 1972. "The Effect of Multicollinearity and Specification Error on Models of Political Behavior." Ph.D. dissertation, University of Michigan, Ann Arbor, MI.

Dilalla, Lisabeth F. 2000. "Structural Equation Modeling: Uses and Issues." Pp. 439-464 in *Handbook of Applied Multivariate Statistics and Mathematical Modeling* edited by Howard E. A. Tinsley and Steven D. Brown. New York: Academic Press.

Duncan, Otis D. 1966. "Path Analysis: Sociological Example." *American Journal of Sociology* 72 (July): 1-16.

———. 1970. "Partials, Partitions, and Path." Pp.38-47 in *Sociological Methodology*, edited by E. F. Borgatta and G. W. Bohrnstedt. San Francisco: Jossey-Bass.

———. 1975. *Introduction to Structural Equation Models*. New York: Academic Press.

Ducasse, C. J. 1951. *Nature, Mind and Death*. LaSalle lL: Open Court.

Einhorn, H. J., and R. M Hogarth. 1986. "Judging Probable Cause." *Psychological Bulletin* 99:3-19.

Elifson, Kirk W., Richard P. Runyon, and Audrey Haber. 1998. *Fundamentals of Social Statistics*. New York: McGraw Hill Publishing Co.

Farrar, D. E. and R. R, Glauber. 1967. "Multicollinearity in Regression Analysis: The Problem Revisited." *Review of Econometrics and Statistics* 49:92-107.

Feigl, H. and M. Brodbeck. 1953. eds. *Readings in the Philosophy of Science*. New York: Appleton-Century Crofts.

Forbes, H. D. and E. R. Tufte. 1968. "A Note of Caution in Causal Modeling." *American Political Science Review* 62 (December): 1258-1264.

Frankfort-Nachmias, C. and D. Nachmias. 1992. *Research Methods in the Social Sciences*. New York: St. Martins.

Galileo, Galilei. [1638] 1974. *Two New Sciences*. Translated by Stillman Drake. Madison: University of Wisconsin Press.

Gravetter, Frederick J. and Larry B. Wallnau. 2004. Statistics for the Behavioral Sciences. Belmont, CA: Wadsworth/Thomson Learning.

Goldberger, A.S.1970. "On Boudon's Method of Linear Causal Analysis." *American Sociological Review* 25:97-101.

Goldberger, A. S., and O. D. Duncan. eds. 1973. *Structural Equation Models in the Social Sciences*. New York: Seminar Press.

Gordon, R. A. 1967. "Values in the Ecological Study of Delinquency." *American Sociological Review* 32:927-944.

Hanson, N.R.1958. *Patterns of Discovery*. Cambridge: Cambridge University Press.

———. 1971. *Observation and Explanation: A Guide to Philosophy of Science*. New York: Harper and Row.

Hauser, R. M. and A. S. Goldberger. 1971. "The Treatment of Unobservable Variables in Path Analysis." Pp. 81-117 in *Sociological Methodology*, edited by H. L. Costner. San Francisco: Jossey-Bass.

Heise, David R. 1969. "Problems in Path Analysis and Causal Inferences." Pp. 38-73 in *Sociological Methodology*, edited by E. F. Borgatta and C. W. Bohrnstedt. San Francisco: Jossey-Bass.

———. 1971. "Separating Reliability and Stability in Test-Retest Correlation." Pp.348-363 in *Causal Models in the Social Sciences* edited by H. M. Blalock. Chicago: Aldine-Atherton.

———. 1975. *Causal Analysis*. New York: John Wiley and Sons.

Holland, Paul W. 1986. "Statistics and Causal Inference." *Journal of the American Statistical Association* 81: 945-960.

———. 1988. "Causal Inference, Path Analysis, and Recursive Structural Equation Models (with discussion)." Pp. 449-493 in *Sociological Methodology* edited by C. C. Clogg. Washington, DC. American Sociological Association.

Hume, David. [1739] 1978. *A Treatise of Human Nature*. Oxford: Oxford University Press.

———. [1740] 1988. "An Abstract of a Treatise of Human Nature." Pp.29-43 in *An Enquiry Concerning Human Understanding/David Hume: Introduction, Notes, and*

Editorial Arrangement by Anthony Flew edited by A. Flew. La Salle, IL: Open Court.

———. [1748] 1988. "An Enquiry Concerning Human Understanding." Pp.53-195 in *An Enquiry Concerning Human Understanding/David Hume: Introduction, Notes, and Editorial Arrangement by Anthony Flew* edited by A. Flew. La Salle, IL: Open Court.

James, Lawrence R. and K. Singh. 1978. "An Introduction to The Logic, Assumptions, and Basic Analytic Procedures of Two-stage Least Squares." *Psychological Bulletin* 85:1104-1122.

Kant, Immanuel. ([1781] 1961). *Critique of Pure Reason*, 2nd ed. Garden City, New York: Doubleday.

Kerlinger, Fred N. 1973. *Foundations of Behavioral Research*. New York: Holt Rinehart and Winston, Inc.

Kenny, D. A.1979. *Correlation and Causality*. New York: John Wiley

Labovitz, S. 1967. "Some Observations on Measurement and Statistics." *Social Forces* 46 (December): 151-160.

———. 1970. "The Assignment of Numbers to Rank Order Categories." *American Sociological Review* 35 (June): 515- 524.

Land, Kenneth C. 1969. "Principles of Path Analysis." Pp. 3-37 in *Sociological Methodology*, edited by E. F. Borgatta and C. W. Bohrnstedt. San Francisco: Jossey-Bass.

———. 1970. "On the Estimation of Path Coefficients for Unmeasured Variables from Correlation among Observed Variables." *Social Forces* 48:506-511.

———. 1973. "Identification, Parameter Estimation, and Hypothesis Testing in Recursive Sociological Models." Pp.19-49 in *Structural Equation Models in the Social Sciences*, edited by A. S. Goldberger and O. D. Duncan. New York: Seminar Press.

Lerner, D. ed. 1965. *Cause and Effect: The Hayden Colloquium on Scientific Method and Concept*. New York: The Free Press.

Mackie, J. L.1965. "Causes and Conditions." *Am. Phil. Quart.* 2, No. 4 (Oct.): 245-264

———. 1974. *The Cement of the Universe: A Study of Causation*. London: Oxford Press (Clarendon).

Maxim, Paul S. 1999. *Quantitative Research Methods in the Social Sciences*. New York: Oxford University Press.

Mayer, L. S. 1970. "Comment on The Assignment of Number to Rank Order Categories." *American Sociological Review* 35(August): 916-917.

———. 1971. "A Note on Treating Ordinal Data as Interval Data." *American Sociological Review* (June): 519-520.

McClelland, P. D. 1975. *Causal Explanation and Model Building in History, Economics, and The New Economic History*. Ithaca, New York: Cornell University Press.

Mill, John S. [1843] 1973. *A System of Logic: Ratiocinative and Inductive, in The Collected Works of John Stuart Mill Vol. 7* edited by J. M. Robinson. Toronto: University of Toronto Press.

Nagel, E. 1961. *The Structure of Science*. New York: Harcourt, Brace & World.
———. 1965. "Types of Causal Explanation in Science." Pp.11-32 in *Cause and Effect*, edited by D. Lerner. New York: Free Press.
Pedhazur, Elazar J. 1982. *Multiple Regression in Behavioral Research: Explanation and Prediction*. New York: Holt, Rinehart and Winston.
Russell, Bertrand. 1912- 1913. "On the Notion of Cause." *Proc. Aristotelian Society* 13: 1- 26.
Salkind, Neil J. 2003. *Exploring Research*. Upper Saddle River, New Jersey: Prentice Hall.
Schoenberg, R. 1972. "Strategies for Meaningful Comparison." Pp. 1-35 in *Sociological Methodology* edited by H. L. Costner. San Francisco: Jossey Bass.
Scriven, M. 1971. "The Logic of Cause." *Theory and Decision* 2: 49- 66.
———. 1975. "Causation as Explanation." *Nous* 9: 3-16.
Seltiz, Claire, Marie Jahoda, Morton Deutsch, and Stewart W. Cook. 1959. *Research Methods in Social Relations*. Revised edition. New York: Holt, Rinehart and Winston.
Siegel, P. M. and R. W. Hodge.1968. "A Causal Approach to the Study of Measurement Error." Pp. 28-59 in *Methodology in Social Research*, edited by H. M. Blalock. New York: McGraw Hill.
Simon, H. A.1957. *Models of Man*. New York: Wiley.
———. 1968. "Causation." Pp. 350-355 in *International Encyclopedia of the Social Sciences,* edited by D. L. Sills. New York: MacMillian.
Sobel, Michael E. 1990. "Effect Analysis and Causation in Linear Structural Equation Models." *Psychometrika* 55: 495-515.
———. 1995. "Causal Inferences in Social and Behavioral Sciences." Pp.1-32 in *The Handbook of Statistical Modeling for Social and Behavioral Sciences*, edited by Gerhard Arminger, Clifford C. Clogg, and Michael E. Sobel. New York: Plenum Press.
Specht, David A. and R. D. Warren. 1975. "Comparing Causal Models." Pp. 46-82 in *Sociological Methodology* edited by D. R. Heise. San Francisco: Jossey Bass.
Suppes, P. 1970. *A Probabilistic Theory of Causality*. Amsterdam: North Holland.
Turkey, J. W. 1954. "Causation, Regression, and Path Analysis." Pp.35-66 in *Statistics and Mathematics in Biology*, edited by O. Kempthorne et al. Ames: Iowa State College Press.
Turner, M. E. and C. D. Stevens. 1959. "The Regression Analysis in Causal Paths." *Biometrics* 15(June): 236-258.
Uslaner, E. M. 1976. *Regression Analysis: Simultaneous Equation*. Beverly Hills, CA: Sage.
Von Wright, G. H. 1971. *Explanation and Understanding*. Ithaca, New York: Cornell University Press.
———. 1974. *Causality and Determinism*. New York: Columbia University Press.
Wallace, William A. 1972. *Causality and Scientific Explanation.* Vol.1. Ann Arbor: University of Michigan Press.
———. 1974. *Causality and Scientific Explanation.* Vol. 2. Ann Arbor: University of Michigan Press.

Wertz, C. E., K. G. Joreskog, and R. L. Linn. 1973. "Identification and Estimation in Path Analysis with Unmeasured Variables." *American Journal of Sociology* 78 (May):1469-1484.

White, H. J., and R. M. Hogarth. 1990. "Ideas About Causation in Philosophy and Psychology." *Psychological Bulletin* 108:3-18.

Wiley, E. D. 1973. "The Identification Problem for Structural Equation Models with Unmeasured Variables." Pp.69-83 in *Structural Equation Model in the Social Sciences*, edited by A. S. Goldberger and O. D. Duncan. New York: Seminar Press.

Wiley, D. E. and J. A. Wiley. 1971. "The Estimation of Measurement Error in Panel Data." Pp.364-374 in *Causal Models in the Social Sciences*, edited by H. M. Blalock. Chicago: Aldine-Atherton.

Wilson, J. Q. and R. J. Hernstein. 1985. *Crime and Human Nature*. New York: Simon & Schuster.

Wilson,T. P. 1971. "Critique of Ordinal Variables." Pp.415-431 in *Causal Models in the Social Sciences*, edited by H. M. Blalock. Chicago: Aldine-Atherton.

Wonnacott, R. J. and T. H. Wonnacott. 1970. *Econometrics*. New York: Wiley.

Wright, Sewall. 1921. "Correlation and Causation." *Journal of Agricultural Research* 20:557-585.

———. 1934. "The Method of Path Coefficients." *Annals of Mathematical Statistics* 5 (September): 161- 215.

———. 1954. "The Interpretation of Multivariate Systems." Pp.11-33 in *Statistics and Mathematics in Biology*, edited by O. Kempthorne etal, Ames: Iowa State College Press.

———. 1960a. "Path Coefficients and Path Regressions: Alternative or Complementary Concepts." *Biometrics* 16 (June):189-202.

———. 1960b. "The Treatment of Reciprocal Interactions, With or Without Lag in Path Analysis." *Biometrics* 16 (September): 423-445.

Young, J. Z. 1978. *Programs of the Brain*. Oxford: Oxford University Press.

Chapter Two

Definition of Basic Terms and Concepts

Causal modeling (path analysis) provides the researcher with a systematic methodology for developing and testing theories. **Path model**, **Path coefficient**, and the other terms and concepts explained below form the basis of communication in path analysis. In order to understand path analysis, it is necessary and useful to know the meanings of some terms and concepts researchers frequently use. This chapter offers a language lesson of sorts. Before continuing, a clear definition of the terms and concepts in path analysis is necessary to help the reader understand subsequent chapters.

Antecedent Variable

A variable that causes spurious relationships between other variables. The source of a spurious relationship is called an antecedent variable because it occurs before the independent and dependent variables. For example, a parent's income (antecedent variable) occurs before type of school (independent variable) and academic achievement of the children (dependent variable) and therefore causes the false relationships between them. This can be shown thus:

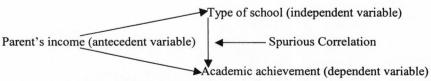

Figure 2.1.   Position of Antecedent Variable.

Rosenberg (1968) states three statistical conditions to determine whether a variable is antecedent or not: All three variables (antecedent, independent, and dependent) must be related; the relationship between independent and dependent variables should not disappear when antecedent variable is controlled; and the relationship between antecedent and dependent variables should disappear when independent variable is controlled.

Assumptions

These are the rules guiding the use of any statistical techniques that researchers must strive to satisfy before applying the techniques to analyze data. Different statistical techniques have different assumptions. The assumptions for path analysis fully discussed in Chapter 4 include: linearity, interval level of measurement, normality, and autocorrelation.

Autocorrelation

This is the correlation between error terms. It occurs when error terms (residuals) from observations of the same variable at different times are correlated. In regression analysis, it is assumed that error terms do not correlate with each other so as to specify a model in which there is only one predictive force (independent variable) affecting the dependent variable. See Chapter 4 for more discussion.

Beta Coefficient

This is a standardized regression coefficient indicating the amount of net change in a dependent variable associated with an increase (or decrease) in one standard deviation in an independent variable when controlling the effect of other independent variables. It is also called un-standardized regression coefficient (b) and beta weight (β). It can be obtained by multiplying b by the ratio of the standard deviation of the independent variable to get the dependent variable:

$$\beta_1 = (S_1/sy)\, b_1$$

Beta coefficient translates the variables to a uniform scale so that it is easy to compare the relative strength of the independent variable with the dependent variable even if the variables to which they apply were measured on a very different scale. For example, the beta weights given to variables such as intelligence, grade point average, and socio-economic status (which are all measured on different nonequivalent scales) can be directly compared, whereas the b weights cannot.

Beta Weight

This is another term for standardized regression coefficient. It enables researchers to compare the size of influence of independent variables measured using different metrics or scales of measurement.

Causal Conclusion

This is a conclusion drawn from a study designed in such a way that it is legitimate to infer cause. It is mostly used in experimental research design in which subjects are randomly assigned to experimental and control groups. It is called causal conclusion because it is only in experimental research design that one can conclude that the effect is caused by the independent variables in the experiment while controlling for all extraneous variables.

Causal Modeling

A causal model is an abstract quantitative representation of real-world dynamics. It attempts to describe the causal relationship among a set of variables. A causal model can be represented in a path diagram, which is a pictorial representation of the theoretical explanations of the cause and effect relationship among the variables. For example, the causal relationships among a father's education (X_1), a mother's education (X_2), children's education (X_3), and children's occupation (X_4) can be represented diagrammatically thus:

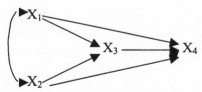

Figure 2.2.   Diagram of a Causal Modeling

It is also represented in structural equation form, and is typically stated in its standard form in which the causal effects are represented by "P" coefficients e.g. $Z_1 = P_{41}Z_1 + P_{42}Z_2 + P_{43}Z_3 + e_4$.

Causal Relationship

This is a relationship in which one variable directly or indirectly influences another or a relationship in which changes in the value of one variable cause changes in the value of another. Causal relationship can be recursive (unidirectional), in which case variable A influences variable B, A $\longrightarrow$ B, but not vice versa. It can also be non-recursive, in which each variable influences the other, A $\longleftrightarrow$ B. Other forms of causal relationship include Figure 2.3a. $X_1 \longrightarrow X_2.$ Here independent variable (X_1) causes changes in dependent variable (X_2).

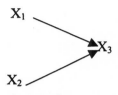

Figure 2.3b.
Uncorrelated Causes

Here, two variables $(X_1$ and $X_2)$ influence X_3. The model suggests that variation in the dependent variable (X_3) has multiple causes. That is, uncorrelated variables $(X_1$ and $X_2)$ contribute to changes in the value of X_3.

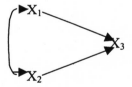

Figure 2.3c.
Correlated Variables

In this situation, two correlated variables $(X_1$ and $X_2)$ cause changes in the value of X_3. The curved, double headed arrows between X_1 and X_2 indicate a correlational relationship, not a causal relationship.

Causation

A situation in which a change in one variable produces a change in another variable. Causation can take place between variables when the following conditions are present: If one variable changes, the other variable must change also; there is a temporal order between the variables- that is, one variable must precede the other in time- and no other or third variable should be able to explain the association between the two variables. Causation is not correlation, in that causation shows that a change in one variable causes a change in another, whereas correlation shows that the two variables are associated but not causally related.

Causal Chain Model

A causal model in which a sequence of events leads ultimately to variation in the dependent variable. A simple causal chain model is illustrated thus:

$$X_1 \longrightarrow X_2 \longrightarrow X_3;$$
$$X_1 \longrightarrow X_2 \longrightarrow X_3 \longrightarrow X_4 \, .$$

Example of a complex causal chain model:

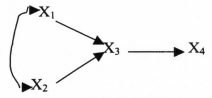

Figure 2.4. Complex Causal Chain

Coefficient

A number used as a measure of a property or characteristic.

Coefficient of Determination

Also called index of association. It is a statistic that indicates how much of the variance in one variable is determined or explained by one or more other variables and how much the variance in one is associated with variance in the others. It is abbreviated r^2 in bivariate analyses and R^2 in multivariate analyses. For example, $r^2 = .22$ may be interpreted as "education level attained", which explains 22% of adults' occupational status. R^2 indicates the proportion of variation in the dependent variable that is explained by a set (or combination) of independent variables. $R^2 = .22$ can be interpreted as about 22% of the variance in the dependent variable is explained by all independent variables in the model.

Co-linear

Having a common line.

Common Cause

This is the causal relationship of one exogenous variable on two endogenous variables. For example, in the diagram below, a common cause can be obtained by tracing backward from X_4 to X_1 to obtain P_{41} and then forward to X_3 to obtain P_{31}. This compound path due to X_1 as a common cause yields: $P_{41}P_{31}$

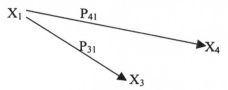

Figure 2.5.   A Common Cause

Confounding Variable

A variable that systematically varies along with the independent variable or that obscures the effect of another. As an example, imagine that a physics instructor wants to know whether a new teaching method works better than the traditional method used with students in an advanced physics course. The instructor used the new method for the morning section of the course and the traditional method for the afternoon section. The instructor used the same textbook, covered the same material, and gave the same tests in both sections. The results show that the students in the section in which the new method was used earned better grades than those in the section taught by the traditional method. Based on these results, the instructor concludes that the new method is better for teaching advanced physics. This conclusion is not justified because other possible (confounding) variables that might have improved the grade have not been eliminated. For example, students in the morning section might be more alert than in the afternoon, the instructor might have more energy to teach better in the morning than in the afternoon, the instructor might be more enthusiastic when using the new method because it was expected to work better, or the students in the morning section might be more motivated than those in the afternoon class.

Control for

A procedure to eliminate alternative sources of variation that may distort the research results. It is one of the criteria of causality that require that the researcher rules out other factors that can invalidate the inference that variables are causally related. Methods of control include: holding variables constant under experimental conditions by setting up an experimental group and a control group; setting up a research design, in part, to maximize systematic variance, minimize error variance, and control extraneous variance; matching subjects; subject selection; assigning subjects randomly to experimental groups; testing alternative hypotheses to the hypothesis under study; or using statistical control such as partialing to identify, isolate, or nullify variance in a dependent variable that is caused by the extraneous variables.

Correlation

The extent to which two or more variables are related to one another. This is usually expressed as a correlation coefficient.

Correlation Coefficient

A measure of association between two continuous variables that estimates the direction and strength of a linear relationship. The direction of the relationship may be positive $(+)$ or negative (inverse) or $(-)$. Although no established rule specifies what constitutes a weak, moderate, or strong relationship, according to Elifson, Runyon and Haber (1998) these general guidelines used by many researchers may be useful: a weak relationship, $r = \pm 0.01$ to ± 0.30; a moderate relationship, $r = \pm 0.31$ to ± 0.70; and a strong relationship, $r = \pm 0.71$ to ± 0.99. A perfect relationship is $r = \pm 1.00$, and no relationship is indicated where $r = 0$. Many statistical techniques can be used to compute correlation coefficients including Pearson's product-moment, Spearman's Rho, and Kendall's Tau.

Correlated Cause

This is a non-causal effect of one independent variable on a dependent variable due to its correlation with another independent variable (a third variable) which has a direct effect on the dependent variable. In the diagram below, the correlated cause between X_1 and X_3 can be obtained by tracing backward from X_3 to X_2 to obtain direct effect (P_{32}), and then forward to X_1 to obtain the correlation (r_{12}). Then the coefficient values of the direct effect (P_{32}) and correlation (r_{12}) should be multiplied to obtain $P_{32}r_{12}$. The correlated cause of X_1 on X_3 is $P_{32}r_{12}$. That is, X_1 is related to X_3 due to its correlation with X_2.

Figure 2.6.   Correlated Cause Between X₁ and X₃

Correlated Effect

A component in the decomposition of a correlation coefficient that is due to a correlation among predetermined variables.

Correlated Variables

These are variables that are assumed to correlate but are not causally related. They are placed at the same point on the horizontal axis of the causal diagram and linked by a curved, double-headed arrow indicating a correlation between them. In the diagram below, X_1 and X_2 are correlated variables in that X_1 does not cause changes in X_2 and vice versa. The coefficient value (r_{12}) of their correlation only indicates the strength of their relationship but not the causal relationship between them.

Figure 2.7.   Correlated Variables

Correlation Matrix

A summary table of correlation coefficients that shows all pairs of relations of a set of variables, R, a correlation matrix, R, is a square, symmetrical matrix. In a correlation matrix, each row and each column represents a different variable, and the value at the intersection of each row and column is the correlation between the two variables. For instance, in the table below, the value (**0.33**) at the intersection of the second row, third column is the correlation between the second (X_2) and the third (X_3) variables. The same correlation (**0.33**) also appears at the intersection of the third row, second column.

The diagonal of a correlation matrix represents the correlation of a variable with itself; therefore, all of the values on the diagonal are **1.00**. That is why the correlation matrices are said to be symmetrical about the main diagonal. That is, they are mirror images of themselves above and below the diagonal going from top left to bottom right. Because each row in the matrix represents the correlation of a specific variable with other variables, as does each column, it is a common practice to show only the bottom half or the top half of an R matrix. Pearson correlation coefficients are used for a correlation matrix. See table below for an example of a correlation matrix.

Table: 2.1.   Correlation Matrixes of Hypothetical Data.

	X_1	X_2	X_3	X_4
X_1	**1.00**	0.02	−0.19	−0.23
X_2	0.02	**1.00**	**0.33**	0.50
X_3	−0.19	**0.33**	**1.00**	0.40
X_4	−0.23	0.50	0.40	**1.00**

Co-variation

The extent to which two variables vary together. That is, if there is a systematic change in one variable, there must be a systematic change in the other. If X changes, Y must also change. It is one of the conditions for causation.

Path Decomposition

The breaking down of correlation coefficients between an exogenous and an endogenous variable, or between two endogenous variables, into different parts: direct effects, indirect effects, unanalyzed correlations, and spurious correlations. For example, X_1 and X_2 are exogenous variables, whereas X_3 is an endogenous variable in this path diagram:

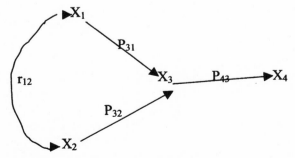

Figure 2.8.   Parts of Path Decomposition

The correlation between X_1 and X_2 (r_{12}) is treated as "given" and can therefore not be decomposed, but the correlation between X_1 and X_3, X_2 and X_3, and X_3 and X_4 can be decomposed into direct effects. The correlation between X_1, X_3 and X_4; X_2, X_3 and X_4 can be decomposed into indirect effects. Utilizing path decomposition is imperative because correlation coefficients can be decomposed into the following components: direct effects, indirect effects, unanalyzed correlation and spurious correlation due to common causes. For a detailed illustration of this concept, see the path decomposition table in Chapter 5.

Deterministic Model

A causal model that contains no random or probability elements, one in which all causes and values are known and all the variance in the dependent variables can be explained.

Deterministic Relationship

A causal relationship in which change in one variable always produces a constant change in another variable.

Direct Effects

The influence of one variable on another that is not mediated by any other variable in a model. $A \rightarrow B$.

Effect Coefficient

The total effect (i.e. direct plus indirect) of an independent variable on a dependent variable. See total effect.

Endogenous Variable

(dependent variable): A variable whose variation is explained by an exogenous (independent) variable in the system. It is a variable that is an inherent part of the system being studied and that is determined from within the system. It is a variable that is caused by other variables in the causal system. For example, in the figure below, X_3 and X_4 are endogenous variables; X_1 and X_2 are exogenous variables.

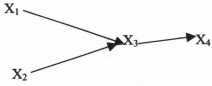

Figure 2.9.   Positioning Endogenous Variables

Epistemic Relationship

The relationship between abstract, theoretical (unobserved) concepts and their corresponding operational (observed) measurements.

Error term

This is part of an equation indicating what is unexplained by the independent variables. It specifies how big the unexplained part is. It is also called the "residual" or "disturbance term" because it is what is left over after one subtracts from the total variance in the dependent variable the part that can be explained by the independent variables. The placement of error term is shown in the path diagram below:

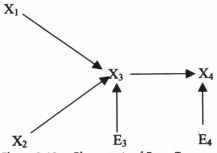

Figure 2.10.   Placements of Error Terms

E is the symbol used for error term. It is assumed that a residual variable is not correlated with other residuals or with independent variables. E is the square root of the unexplained variation in the dependent variable under analysis ($\sqrt{1 - R^2}$).

Exogenous Variable (independent variable):

A variable whose variation is to be determined by causes outside the causal model and which also affects the endogenous variable. This variable is not correlated with the residuals. In causal analysis, exogenous variables must be placed before endogenous variables. Whether a variable is designated the exogenous variable or the endogenous variable is determined by its usage. That is a variable must be placed into a framework or research situation before it can be designated as either exogenous or endogenous. Symbolically, an exogenous variable is represented by X, and an endogenous one by Y, but conventionally, letter X in path analysis can represent any variable. For example, father's education (X_1, exogenous variable) → children's education (X_2, endogenous variable).

External Specification Problem

The condition in which to consider whether a particular exogenous (input) variable or set of variables should be included in the model.

Fully Recursive Model

This is a recursive path analysis model in which all variables are connected by arrows. That is, all variables are causally linked. It is also called " just identified model". This is an example of a fully recursive model:

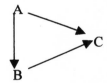

Figure 2.11.   Fully recursive Model

Goodness of Fit

This explains how well a model or theoretical distribution matches actual data. A goodness of fit criterion measures the quality of the model.

Goodness of Fit Tests

These are statistical techniques to determine whether our model match data. Examples of goodness of fit tests discussed in the book include Chi Square and F-test.

Heteroskedasticity

A situation in which there are considerably unequal variances in the two or more population distributions. Heteroskedasticity is either caused by non-normality of one of the variables or by the fact that one variable is related to some transformation of the other. Heteroskedasticity is one of the assumptions discussed in Chapter 4.

Heuristic Device

An artificial construct that is used to assist in understanding. For example, Weber's "ideal type" is a heuristic device in sociology.

Homoskedasticity

A condition in which the variances of two or more population distributions are equal. It purports that the variability in scores for one continuous variable is roughly the same for another continuous variable. It is related to the assumption of normality because when the assumption of normality is met, the relationship between the variables is homoskedastic. This assumption is fully discussed in Chapter 4.

Identification Problem

An analytic difficulty that arises in regression analysis when one has more unknowns than can be independently estimated from the available data. That is, too many unknowns in a causal model exist for a solution to be possible. The problem arises because the combined forces of the theory and data constraints are insufficient to determine unique estimates of the structural coefficients.

Indirect Effect

This is the effect of one variable on another through at least one other variable in a model. The effect of one variable on another mediated through a third intervening variable is illustrated thus:

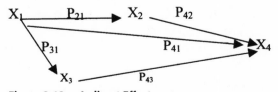

Figure 2.12.   Indirect Effects

Indirect effect can be estimated by multiplying the path coefficients of path connecting two variables via intervening variables. In this diagram the indirect effect of X_1 on X_4 via X_2 would be expressed by $P_{21}P_{42}$, and the indirect effect of X_1 on X_4 via X_3 would be $P_{31}P_{43}$.

Instrumental Variable

An exogenous variable that affects only one of the endogenous variables involved in a reciprocal relationship. It is a variable included in a model to make non-recursive model identified. In the diagram below variable, X, is an instrumental variable for Y in the non recursive relationship Y ⟷ Z because of the conditions specified by Heise (1975):

a. X has no direct effect on Z;
b. X affects Y, either directly or through an intervening variable that has no direct effect on Z;
c. Neither Y nor Z has a direct or indirect effect on X;
d. No unspecified factor jointly affects X and Z, and, in general, X is uncoordinated with the disturbances of Z
   Example: X Y Z

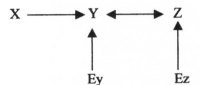

Figure 2.13.   Placement of Instrumental Variable

Interaction Effect

This is the joint effect of two or more independent variables on a dependent variable. It occurs when independent variables not only have separate effects but also have combined effects on a dependent variable. An example of interaction effect occurs when two or more drugs are taken simultaneously. Mixing drugs may have the effect of both added together plus an "extra" effect resulting from combination of the two. This extra effect is the interaction effect.

Internal Specification

The process of specifying the direct and indirect effects of independent variables upon the dependent and intervening variables.

Internal Specification Error

The question of whether a particular path should be included in the model or not.

Intervening Variable

A variable in between the exogenous and endogenous variables. It is the variable through which the exogenous variable indirectly affects the endogenous variable. For example, the statistical association between two parents' education (the father's education, X_1 and the mother's education, X_2) and the children's occupation (X_4) needs to be explained, because educational achievement of the parents by itself does not make the children get a good job. Other variables intervene between the parents' education and the children's occupation. For instance, children from an educated family may be more motivated to get good education than those from an uneducated family. Children's education (X_3) is an intervening variable because it mediates the relationship between the parents' education and the children's occupation. This is graphically shown thus:

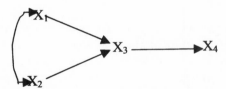

Figure 2.14. **Placement of Intervening Variable**

Inverse Correlation

A relation between two variables such that, whenever one goes up the other goes down, and vice versa. It is also called negative correlation (-). For example, if the correlation between female employment and fertility rate is $r = -.25$, it means the female employment rate increases by 25% and the fertility rate decreases by 25% or vice versa.

Just-Identified Model

This is a model in which the number of equations is equal to the number of parameters that are to be estimated (no paths deleted), therefore affording a unique solution for each of them. That is the number of βs that can be uniquely estimated is equal to the number of path coefficients that are to be estimated. A recursive model is just identified when all the variables are interconnected either by curved lines (among the exogenous variables) or by paths (among the exogenous and the endogenous variables, and among the endogenous variables themselves), and the assumptions about the residuals are tenable. Below is an example of a just-identified model:

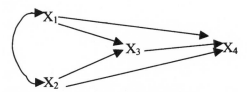

Figure 2.15.   Just-Identified Model

In just-identified, or exactly identified causal model it is possible to reproduce R, regardless of how questionable, or even bizarre, the causal model may be on substantive or logical grounds.

Measurement Error

This is inaccuracy in measurement due to flaw in a measuring instrument. For example, if a researcher studying the effects of stress on blood pressure used faulty pressure gauge this would lead to measurement error. The true value of the blood pressure could be obtained if the measuring instrument were not faulty; unfortunately, the gauge may be faulty and therefore estimate the true value of the blood pressure by obtaining an observed value. The difference between the true value of a variable (blood pressure) and the observed value is the error of measurement. This can be shown thus: True Value − Observed Value = Measurement Error

Measurement error is one of the assumptions discussed in chapter 4.

Misspecification

A condition in which a structural equation or path model includes incorrect variables or excludes correct variables. Misspecification is fully discussed in Chapter4.

Model

A representation or description of something (a phenomenon or set of relationships) that aids in understanding or studying it. The purpose of constructing a model is to test it. A model can be a graphical causal model as shown below:

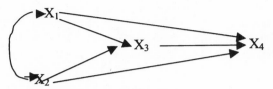

Figure 2.16. Diagram of a Model

It can also be an equation form that states a theory in formal, symbolic language, as in a regression equation $Yi = a + b_1x_1 + b_2x_2 + b_3x_3 \ldots + bexe$. A model requires the researcher to engage with theory and thus avoid empiricism. A model seeks to simplify phenomena, as an aid to conceptualization and explanation.

Single-Equation Causal Model is a model in which the independent variables are correlated (not causally related) with causal effects on one dependent variable:

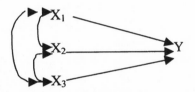

Figure 2.17. Single-Equation Model

The equation for the model is:

$$\hat{Y} = a + b_1x_1 + b_2x_2 + b_3x_3$$

A Two-Equation Causal Model is a single model in which the diagram specifies two separate causal equations:

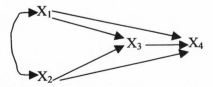

Figure 2.18. Two-equation Model

The two separate equations are:

$$X_3 = a + b_1x_1 + b_2x_2$$
$$X_4 = a + b_1x_1 + b_2x_2 + b_3x_3$$

A Three-Equation Causal Model is a model that shows causal effect between one independent variable and three dependent variables:

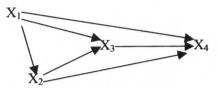

Figure 2.19.   Three-equation Model

The three separate equations are:

$$X_2 = a + b_1x_1$$
$$X_3 = a + b_1x_1 + b_2x_2$$
$$X_4 = a + b_1x_1 + b_2x_2 + b_3x_3$$

Necessary Condition

In causal analysis, a variable or event that must be present for another variable or event to occur. This is one of the conditions in causal relationships. It shows a variable (X) is necessary for the existence of another variable (Y). That is, X must occur before Y can occur. Even though X is necessary for the existence of Y it may not be sufficient for the existence of Y. This means that X is a partial cause of Y. It combines with other factors to cause Y to occur. For example research may show that smoking may cause lung cancer but not everybody who smokes suffers from lung cancer. Actually, only those smokers who also live in a smog-filled area (Z) will get cancer. This shows that smoking is necessary for getting cancer, but by itself cannot lead to cancer unless done in combination with the presence of smog.

Nonlinear Relationship

A relationship between two variables, which, when plotted on a graph, does not form a straight line. In nonlinear or curvilinear relationships the rate at which one variable changes in value may be different for different values of the second variable. For example, nonlinear relationship between income (Y) and education (X) is graphically shown below using hypothetical data:

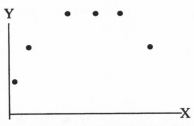

Figure 2.20.   Nonlinear Relationship

This shows a relationship in which Y (Income) varies much more slowly for high values of X (Education) than for low values of X. For example, the relationship between education and income can be nonlinear or curvilinear. Up to a certain point, additional education has marginal utility. That is, to go to school forever would certainly not make one a millionaire.

Non-spuriousness

A non-spurious relation is a relation between two variables that is not due to the effect of a third variable. If the effects of all relevant variables are controlled for and the relation between the original two variables is maintained, the relation is non spurious. A non-spurious relationship shows a strong evidence of an inherent causal link between variables and that the observed co-variation is not based on an accidental connection with some associated phenomena.

Normal Equations

The algebraic equations used in the estimation of linear regression coefficient values. These equations contain the coefficients of correlation among all the independent variables and between the independent variables and the dependent variables and a set of beta weights, βj

$$\hat{Y} = a + b_1 x_1 + b_2 x_2 + b_3 x_3 \ldots\ldots + b_n x_n.$$

Non-recursive Model

A model in which causal influences between variables are reciprocal. A↔B or errors in equations are correlated. In a non-recursive model there is a feedback loop among the variables. That is, there are two lines linking the factors, one with an arrow in one direction and the other line with an arrow in the other direction. Correlated disturbances are linked by single curved lines with double headed arrows. A non-recursive model occurs when there are feedback loops among the dependent variables or there are correlated disturbances among the dependent variables, or both, as shown below:

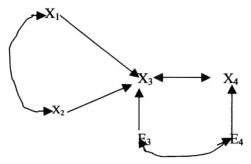

Figure 2.21.   Non-recursive Model

In this model a reciprocal relationship exists between X_3 and X_4 in that X_3 predicts X_4 and X_4 predicts X_3; the error terms, (E_3 and E_4) are linked by a single curved lines with double- headed arrows.

Over identified Model

A model that consists of more equations than are necessary for the purpose of parameter estimation (some paths deleted). An example of over identified model is shown thus:

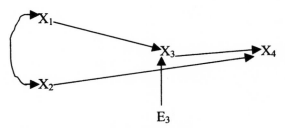

Figure 2.22.   Over-identified Model
No direct paths from X_1 to X_4 and X_2 to X_3

To calculate path coefficient in the over identified model above, regress X_3 on X_1 to obtain $P_{31} = \beta_{31} = r_{13}$. Regress X_4 on X_2 and X_3 to obtain P_{42} and P_{43}. This means that the model contains more information than is necessary to estimate the path coefficients. There are three knowns (the correlation, r, among the three variables) and two unknowns (the two path coefficients, Ps).

P Is the symbol for a path coefficient usually written with two subscripts (pij), the first one (i) indicating the effect (or the dependent variable), and the second subscript (j) indicating the cause (the independent variable). For example, P_{32} indicates the direct effect of variable X_2 on variable X_3. This is graphically shown thus:

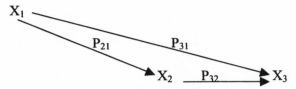

Figure 2.23.   Placement of Path Coefficients (Ps)

Path Analysis

This is a statistical technique that uses both bivariate and multiple linear regression techniques to test the causal relations among the variables specified in the model. Path analysis involves three major steps: The researcher (i) draws a path diagram based on a theory or a set of hypotheses, then (ii) calculates path coefficients (direct effects) using regression technique, and (iii) finally determines the indirect effects. The causal connections are conceived as unidirectional and presented in a path diagram. In essence, therefore, the technique is merely a diagrammatic representation of a set of regression equations for which the variables are assumed to have a temporal ordering. A hypothetical example is provided in the diagram below, which indicates causal relationships between a father's education (X_1), a mother's education (X_2), children's education (X_3), and children's occupation (X_4).

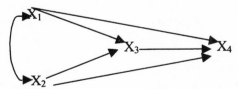

Figure 2.24.   Path Analysis Diagram

Path Coefficients

These are numerical estimates of the causal relationships between variables in a path analysis. They are interpreted as the amount of expected changes in the dependent variables due to a unit change in the independent variable. Coefficients are represented by symbols Pij, "i" being the dependent variable and "j" the independent variable. That is, path coefficients can read P_{21}, P_{31} etc. when numerical values are unknown but specified by theory. For example P_{31} (.32) is the path coefficient connecting X_1 with X_3, with X_3 being determined by X_1. Similarly E_3 (.65) is the path coefficient linking X_3 with the residual variable E. The regression equations for the structure of the model must have as many equations as the number of dependent variables. Illustration:

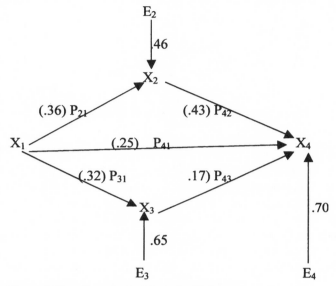

Figure 2.25.   Hypothetical Path Coefficients

$X_2 = P_{21}X_1 + P_{2E}$
$X_3 = P_{31}X_1 + P_{3E}$
$X_4 = P_{41}X_1 + P_{42}X_2 + P_{43}X_3 + P_{4E}$

The equation includes as many terms as there are arrows leading to the dependent variable. Thus X_4 has four arrows, each representing a determining factor X_1, X_2, X_3, and E. Path coefficients can be obtained by regressing each dependent variable on the independent variable in the equation. For example to estimate P_{21}, regress X_2 on X_1. For P_{31}, regress X_3 on X_1, and for P_{41}, P_{42}, P_{43}, regress X_4 on X_1, X_2, and X_3. The path coefficients are simply the beta weights for each equation, that is $P_{21} = \beta_{21}; P_{31} = \beta_{31}; P_{41} = \beta_{41}; P_{42} = \beta_{42}; P_{43} = \beta_{43}$.

Path Diagram

A pictorial representation of the cause-effect relationships among variables using keyword names and direct arrows. A path diagram is guided by some assumptions: a single headed arrow represents the causal order between two variables, with the head pointing to the effect and the tail to the cause e.g. $X_1 \longrightarrow X_2$. It rules out two-way causation either directly in the form $X_1 \longleftrightarrow X_2$ or indirectly as shown thus:

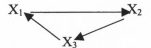

**Figure 2.26.   Diagram of
Indirect Two-way
Causation**

That is, a dependent variable cannot cause any of the variables preceding it in
the causal sequence. For example, if X_1 is the independent variable, X_2 the intervening variable, and X_3 the dependent variable, then X_2 cannot cause X_1,
and X_3 cannot cause X_2 or X_1. Another assumption is that error-terms are not
correlated with each other or with the independent variable and variables that
are correlated and not causally related (e.g. X_1, X_2) should be at the same
point on the horizontal axis of the diagram and linked by a curved double
headed arrows as shown below:

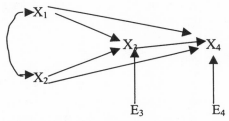

**Figure 2.27.   Path Diagram with
Uncorrelated Error Terms**

Input Path Diagram

This is a path diagram drawn before performing any statistical analysis,
which helps in planning the analysis. It represents the causal connections that
are predicted by hypothesis. Below is an example of input path diagram:

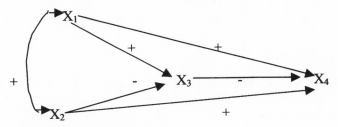

Figure 2.28.   Input Path Diagram

Output Path Diagram

An output path diagram represents the results of a statistical analysis and shows what was actually found. An output path diagram may look like this:

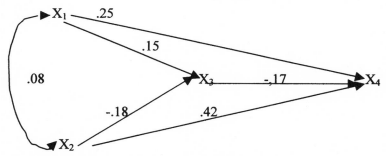

Figure 2.29.   Output Path Diagram of Hypothetical Data

Path Regression Coefficient is another term for an un-standardized regression coefficient in a path analysis.

Predetermined Variables

Variables in a path analysis, the cause or causes of which are not specified in the model. Predetermined variables are usually connected with curved, double-headed arrow and placed at the same point on the horizontal axis of the causal diagram as shown thus:

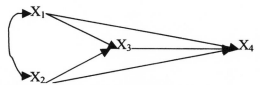

Figure 2.30.   Placement of Predetermined Variables

X_1 and X_2 are predetermined variables, but X_3 and X_4 are not predetermined because they are being determined by X_1 and X_2.

Recursive Model

A model in which all causal influences are supposed to point to one and only one direction (unidirectional) A→B but not A↔B. If A affects B, B must not also affect A in the same model. A relation between two variables is called recursive if it is linear, if the two variables are not in a loop, if the independent variable is uncorrelated with disturbances of dependent variable, and the error terms in the equations are uncorrelated. If all the causal relations in a system are recursive, the entire system is said to be recursive. An example of a recursive model is shown below:

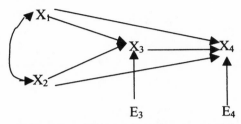

Figure 2.31.   Diagram of a Recursive Model

Residual (error term; disturbance term)

A variable outside the model that is assumed not to correlate with other residuals and with any of the proceeding exogenous variables upon which residuals affect. See **error term**.

Scatter Plot or Scatter Diagram

A plot used to display correlational data from two measures. Each point represents the two scores provided by each subject, one for each measure plotted against one another. Scatter plot allows for a visual inspection of the relationship between the two variables shown in the hypothetical diagrams below:

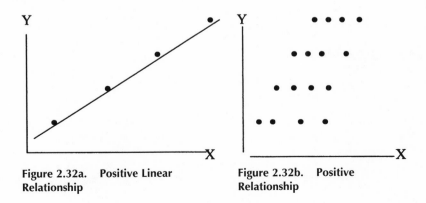

Figure 2.32a.   Positive Linear Relationship

Figure 2.32b.   Positive Relationship

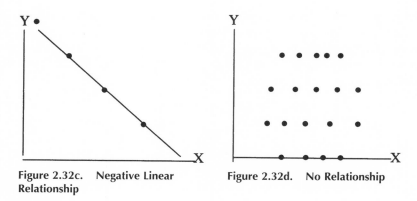

Figure 2.32c. Negative Linear   **Figure 2.32d. No Relationship**
Relationship

The pattern of the points indicates the strength and direction of the correlation between the two variables. The more the points tend to cluster around a straight line, the stronger the relation or the higher the correlation (Figure 2.32a). If the line around which the points cluster runs from lower left to upper right, the relation is positive or direct (Figure 2.32b); if it runs from upper left to lower right, the relation is negative or inverse (Figure 2.32c). If the dots are scattered randomly throughout the grid, there is no relationship between the two variables (Figure 2.32d).

Specification Error

This is a mistake committed by researchers when deciding upon causal model in a regression analysis. Examples of specification error are omitting relevant variables from the regression equation, including irrelevant variables, postulating a linear model when a nonlinear model is more appropriate, or postulating an additive model even though non-additive model is more appropriate. All these refer to a situation in which the researcher enunciated a theoretical model that describes the manner in which the independent variables affect the dependent variables. Specification error is one of the assumptions of path analysis fully discussed in Chapter 4.

Specification Problem

The problem of deciding which variables to include and which to exclude in a regression equation.

Spurious Relationship

A relationship between two variables that is caused by a third variable:

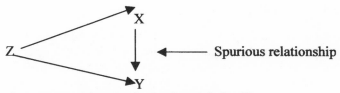

Figure 2. 33.   Diagram of a Spurious Relationship

Variable Z is the spurious variable because variable X and Y appear to be related only because variable Z causes both variables.

Standardized Regression Coefficients, βs

This is the expected change in the dependent variable expressed in standard score, associated with a one standard deviation change in an independent variable, while holding other variables constant. βs are compared across different variables. See **Beta coefficient**

Statistical Significance

Test of significance tells us the existence of any relationship between variables. A value or a measure of a variable has statistical significance when it is "significantly" larger or smaller than would be expected by chance alone. Statistical significance does not necessarily imply substantive or practical significance. A large sample size very often leads to results that are statistically significant, even when they might be otherwise quite inconsequential. A statistically significant relationship exists if there is a real relationship between these variables in the population from which the sample was selected, and no statistical significance indicates no real relationship between the variables, and any relationship found between these variables in the sample occurred just by chance because of sampling error. When a statistically significant relationship exists, users or researchers reject the null hypothesis of no relationship between the variables. This shows that we are making a decision that there is a relationship between the two variables. If the relationship is not statistically significant, it means no relationship between the variables exists. Therefore, we accept the null hypothesis that there is no relationship between two variables.

Structural Equation

A mathematical equation representing the structure of hypothesized relationship among variables in a social theory.

Structural Equation Models

These are models made up of more than one structural equation describing causal relations among latent variables, and include coefficients for endogenous variables. They are used for testing carefully delineated models based on hypothesis about how observed and latent variables are interrelated in order to meaningfully explain the observed relations among the variables in the most parsimonious way. Structural equation modeling is useful because it allows researchers to use a path analysis to test a set of relations among variables simultaneously, by regressing a variable on several other variables, and can in turn simultaneously predict another outcome. This can not be done by using standard regression analysis. It can be used to test factor analysis models, both in an exploratory framework as well as a confirmatory one. It can also be used to assess the applicability of a given model on more than one group, to make direct comparisons between groups, to run growth curve models, and to compare nested models

Substantive Significance

This is said of a research finding when it reveals something meaningful about the object of study. It is often used in contrast with statistical significance, which is present when a finding is unlikely to be due to chance alone.

Sufficient Condition

In causal analysis, a variable or event (X) is sufficient for the existence of another variable or event (Y) if Y occurs every time that X occurs. It is an alternate cause of an event. It can cause an event to happen on its own. Another factor can cause the event to happen too. For example if smoking is sufficient to cause cancer, cancer will exist whenever there is smoking. It needs not combine with other factors. Also smog is sufficient to cause cancer if cancer exists whenever there is smog and is not combined with other factors.

Suppressor Variable

A third variable that makes the relationship between two variables that are actually related appear to be unrelated because the third variable is positively correlated with one of the variables in the relationship and negatively correlated with the other. The relationship between the two variables will reappear when the suppressor variable is controlled for.

Theory Trimming

This is a method of deleting paths whose coefficients are not statistically significant. When path coefficients for a just- identified model is calculated, the researcher may decide to delete some paths in order to offer a more parsimonious causal model, i.e., he conceives of the correlation between the two variables whose connecting path is deleted as being due to indirect effects only. In deleting paths, the following criteria must be taken into account: (a) The primary guideline is the theory of the researcher. The researcher must use a sound theory and previous research in his decision that there is no direct path connecting the two variables in a model. (b) The statistical significance of the path must be considered. Paths whose coefficients are not significant at a specified level e.g. paths with coefficients whose *t* ratios are smaller than the table t at a pre-specified level of significance are deleted. (c) Some researchers may prefer to adopt the criterion of meaningfulness and delete path coefficients they consider not meaningful. What may be meaningful to one researcher in one setting may not be meaningful to another in another setting. Hence, some researchers recommend that path coefficients less than .05 may be treated as non-meaningful

Time Order or Temporal Sequence

This is one of the conditions for causality. It is a necessary condition that changes in an independent variable, which must precede in time the change in the dependent measure, when a causal relationship between the two is assumed. It is assumed in time order that phenomena in the future cannot determine phenomena in the present or the past because it is usually not difficult to determine the time order of phenomena. For example, the status of parents influences the educational expectations of their children. In other cases, however, time order is harder to determine. For example, does achievement follow motivation, or does change in the level of motivation follow achievement? Time order plays a significant role in determining which factor is the cause and which is the effect in that the one that occurs first is the cause and the one that occurs second is the effect.

Total Effect

The sum of the direct and indirect effects. A total effect of an independent variable on a dependent variable is defined as the sum of its direct and indirect effects.

Illustration:

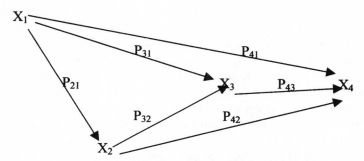

Figure 2.34a.   **Direct Effect and Indirect Effects as Total Effect**

Total effect of X_1 on X_4 is $P_{41} + P_{21}P_{42} + P_{21}P_{32}P_{43} + P_{31}P_{43}$. Depending on the cause, a variable may or may not have a direct effect on another variable. A variable may also have more than one indirect effect on anther variable. When a variable only has a direct effect on another variable, this is the total effect.

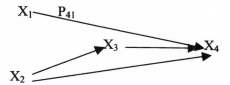

Figure 2.34b.   **Direct Effects as Total Effects**

Total effect of X_1 on X_4 is P_{41}. The total effect of a variable that has no direct effect on another variable is equal to its indirect effect, or the sum of its indirect effects as illustrated below:

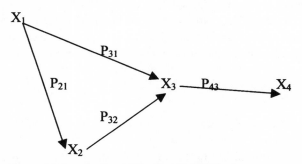

Figure 2.34c.   **Indirect Effects as Total Effect**

Total effect of X_1 on $X_4 = P_{21}P_{32}P_{43} + P_{31}P_{43}$

Unanalyzed Correlation

The correlation between independent variables that is represented by a curved line linking the pair of variables with arrowheads at both ends.

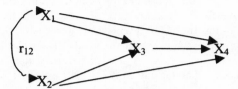

Figure 2.35. Unanalyzed Correlation

Such a link does not represent causal relationship between the variables but correlation or association between the independent variables. The correlation between the independent variables is represented by r_{12} and is generated by calculating Pearson's correlation.

Under-identified Model

A regression model or equation containing too many unknowns to be solved. This model contains insufficient information for the purpose of obtaining a determinate solution of parameter estimation.

Un-standardized Regression Coefficients (b)

Expression of relations between the explanatory and explained variables in terms of the original scales with which these variables were measured.

Zero-order Correlation

A correlation between two variables in which no additional variables have been controlled for.

SUMMARY

This chapter covers the definition of most of the terms and concepts that re-searchers and users of path analysis need in order to apply the technique and interpret their findings. Familiarity with these terms and concepts will pro-vide a foundation for a better understanding of subsequent chapters. The reader is advised to refer back to this chapter if he or she is not sure of the meaning of a certain term or concept. In the next chapter, we will discuss how variables are put together in constructing a causal diagram.

REFERENCES

Allison, Paul D. 1999. *Multiple Regression: A Primer*. Thousand Oaks, CA: Pine Forge Press.

Bordens, Kenneth S. and Bruce B. Abbot. 2002. *Research Design and Methods: A Process Approach*. New York: McGraw Hill.

Elifson, Kirk, Richard P. Runyon, and Audrey Haber. 1998. *Fundamentals of Social Statistics*. New York: McGraw Hill.

Frankfort-Nachmias, Chava and David Nachmias. 2000. *Research Methods in the Social Sciences*. New York: Worth Publishers.

Freund, Rudolf J. and William J. Wilson. 1998. *Regression Analysis: Statistical Modeling of A Response Variable*. San Diego, CA: Academic Press.

Hayduck, Leslie A. 1988. *Structural Equation Modeling with LISREL: Essentials and Advances*. Baltimore, MD: The John Hopkins University Press.

Heise, David R. 1975. *Causal Analysis*. New York: John Wiley & Sons, Inc.

Kerlinger, Fred N. and Elazar J. Pedhazur. 1973. *Multiple Regression in Behavioral Research* . New York: Holt, Rinehart and Winton, Inc.

McClendon, McKee J. 1994. *Multiple Regression and Causal Analysis*. Itasca, IL.: F. E. Peacock Publishers, Inc.

Pedhazur, Elazar J. 1982. *Multiple Regression in Behavioral Research: Explanation and Prediction*. New York: Holt, Rinehart and Winston, Inc.

Rosenberg, Morris. 1968. *The Logic of Survey Analysis*. New York: Basic Books, Inc., Publishers.

Stark, Rodney and Lynne Roberts. 2002. *Contemporary Social Research Methods: A Text Using Microcase*. Belmont, CA: Wadsworth.

Vogt, W. Paul. 1993. *Dictionary of Statistics and Methodology: A Non-technical Guide for The Social Sciences*. Newbury Park, CA: Sage Publications.

Chapter Three

Constructing Causal Diagrams

After selecting the appropriate variables for the study (for example, father's education, mother's education, children's education, and children's occupation) the development of a causal diagram is probably the most difficult aspect of conducting any causal modeling study. Researchers are usually influenced by research literature, personal observations and experience, common sense, logic, and theories among other factors in specifying the model regarding the causal link among the variables. For example, theoretically, it can be stated that the children of educated parents are more likely to be exposed to and motivated toward education at the early age, and their future occupation may be influenced by their education and their parents' education.

Among the factors influencing researchers in model specification, the importance of the role of theory cannot be overstated. In fact, the unique roles of theory in constructing path diagram had been expressed by Bohrnstedt and Carter (1971); MacDonald (1977); Pedhazur (1982); Hanson (1958); Bohrnstedt and Knoke (1982); Bollen and Long (1993); Hetherington (2000). Theory helps researchers to isolate groups of variables into a system of functional equations. Sound theory reduces specification problem because researchers are able to identify relevant variables to be included in the model and irrelevant variables to be excluded, and the conditions under which a causal relationship is likely to exist. Theory not only guides researchers in specifying the logical causal ordering of variables into independent, intervening, and dependent variables but also provides the general framework for investigating the nature of all relationships. Theory plays an important role in interpreting research findings because it is a primary frame of reference through which researchers understand the contents and implications of their findings. It guides researchers in determining how to assess the meaningfulness of a "weak" association and how to test for direction of influence and spuriousness, and the tenability of the model. Such decision rests not on the data, but rather on the theory that generated the causal model in the first place. Theory may also provide us with a statement about the sign (- or +) and/or relative size of the direct effect of one construct on another.

DIAGRAMMING CAUSAL RELATIONSHIPS

In constructing the cause and effect relationship among a set of variables, researchers should take note of the following notational and diagrammatical configurations, assumptions, and conventions that are very important in constructing path diagram (Bohrnstedt and Knoke 1982; Biddle and Marlin 1987; Land 1969; MacDonald 1977; Heise 1975). It is best to include all variables that are theoretically or empirically relevant to the study, and define them clearly because path models require more stringent theoretical specification than multiple regression models. Each variable in the model should be represented by a brief acronym or symbol. According to Heise (1975), conventionally, the following capital letters V, W, X, Y, and Z are reserved for variables. The same letter may be used repeatedly for the variables but can be distinguished by attaching subscripts. For example, if letter X is used, all variables may be identified as X_1, X_2 X_3 etc. but what each acronym, symbol or letter signifies should be clearly defined, *e.g.*, father's education (X_1), mother's education (X_2), children's education (X_3), children's occupation (X_4).

Variable Positioning

The positioning of the variables into a path diagram is very important. Researchers should know the correct ordering of the variables in a path model because it is the most critical assumption that researchers must meet (Land 1969; Kmenta 1971). Researchers should formalize their notion by mapping their ideas onto a path diagram in temporal sequence from left to right. Conventionally, causal models are often drawn in the form of path diagram in which the cause (independent variables) appears on the left, or above the effect (dependent variables) on the right, or below. Intervening variables are scattered in the middle, and dependent variables are placed towards the right. A solid straight line between two variables indicates a direct causal direction while arrowhead pointing from one variable to other shows the direction of causality (MacDonald 1977; Land 1969; Bohrnstedt and Knoke 1982; Duncan 1971; Biddle and Marlin 1987:5; MacCallum 1995). For example,

$X_1 \rightarrow X_3$ means X_1 causes X_3. Collingwood (1940,1948) and Holland (1986) view such temporal priority as an inherent part of causal relation; Sobel (1990) requires that causes should precede effects in time; and Heise (1969:52) states that the causal laws governing the causal priority among variables in the system are un-debatable. Squares or rectangles are used to represent observed or measured variables (MVs) and circles or ellipses to represent unobserved or latent variables (LVs) including error terms (MacCallum 1995; Maxim 1999). Variables assumed to be correlated, but not causally related should be at the same point on the horizontal axis of the causal diagram and linked by a curved double-headed arrow (Bohrnstedt and Knoke 1982; Land 1962; Pedhazur 1982; MacCallum 1995; Maxim 1999).

For example

Figure 3.1.   Correlated Variables

This means variable X_1 and variable X_2 are correlated but not causally related. In some models, some variables may be related to other variables that may lead to multiple causes or effects. Multiple causes occur when many different arrows enter a dependent variable; and multiple effects occur when many arrows come from the same variable (Heise 1975). It is very difficult to position dependent variables with multiple causes or effects. For example variable X_1 may have two dependent variables X_3 and X_4 .By convention (Heise 1975) both dependent variables X_3 and X_4 should be placed to the right, or below X_1 and whether X_3 or X_4, is placed above and to the left of the other should be decided only after all the relations of X_3 and X_4 have been examined. If through examination it were found that X_3 has a causal effect on X_4, then X_3 would be placed above and to the left of X_4 as shown below:

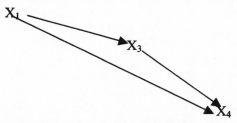

Figure 3.2.   Position of Dependent Variable with Multiple Causes

Following the conventions guiding variable positioning our variables, father's education (X_1), mother's education (X_2), children's education (X_3) and children's occupation (X_4) can be causally entered into a path diagram as follows:

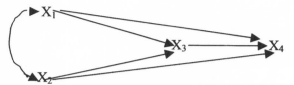

Figure 3.3.   Positioning Variables in Path Diagram

The two independent variables (father's education, X_1 and mother's education, X_2) are at the same point on the left hand side and linked by a curved double-headed arrow because they are only correlated but NOT causally related. Children's education (X_3) precedes children's occupation (X_4) because their parents will expose them to education as they are growing up, and their occupation will follow in their later years. Solid straight lines from X_1 and X_2 to X_3 indicate direct influences on children's education from father's education and mother's education. Solid lines from X_1, X_2, and X_3 on X_4 indicate direct influences on children's occupation from father's education, mother's education, and children's education. Also, father's education and mother's education can indirectly influence children's occupation by going through children's education, which is an intervening variable (intermediate variable).

Path Symbols

After causal paths have been drawn, symbols are entered beside the arrow on a path diagram as path coefficients. The symbols represent a quantitative specification of how a change in one variable makes a change in another. By convention, (Heise 1975; MacCallum 1995; Maxim 1999) the standard symbols used for path coefficients are a, c, d, e, f, g, p, and q (b is reserved for other purposes). Letters with subscripts (e g., *Pij*) or numerical value (such as P_{41}) can be used, where *Pij* represents the path coefficient; "*i*", or the first number denotes the dependent variable; and "*j*" or the second number denotes the independent variable under consideration.

Path coefficient can read a positive relation as P_{21} (+) or negative as P_{21} (−) when numerical values are unknown but specified by theory and when quantitative values are known, and numbers instead of symbols are entered (e g .52 or −.52); r is entered besides the curved double headed arrow between the variables assumed to be correlated but NOT causally related because it represents a correlation coefficient. The μ or E values are representations of residual variance.

To illustrate, Figure 3.4 provides how path coefficient symbols are entered along the arrows of our original path diagram (Figure 3.3).

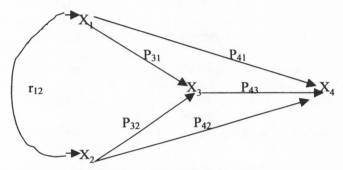

Figure 3.4. Path Diagram Showing Path Coefficients

Error Terms

Researchers should also take into account many factors treated as a single outside source of variable with unknown value. These residual variables or error terms are represented by residual symbols Es or μs to indicate that they are unmeasured. They are also represented by one-way arrow from the residual to the dependent variable (Land 1969; Joreskog and Van Thillo 1972) as shown below:

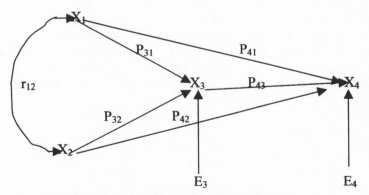

Figure 3.5. Original Path Diagram Showing Error Terms

Figure 3.5 shows that X_3 and X_4 are influenced by X_1 and X_2 but also determined by other unspecified factors, represented jointly as E_3 and E_4. Error terms are included in the diagram because they represent other causes of dependent variables not included in the model (Gujarati 1978:27); a degree of randomness in variability in the responses of individuals or in data collection and coding; and errors in measurement due to imperfect correspondence between construct and operationalizations (Bagozzi 1980:68).

At this time, the diagram is regarded as a heuristic device. It is built up piecemeal by taking two variables at a time and applying the above principles over and over again, adding more variables and more arrows to the diagram, until the researcher is satisfied that it represents the causal sequences based on theory and empirical knowledge about the variables involved. If satisfied with the diagram, the researcher should write the path model or set of recursive equations implied by the diagram.

For instance the equation for Figure 3.5 is written as follows:

$$X_3 = P_{31}X_1 + P_{32} X_2 + P_3 \text{ EXE}$$
$$X_4 = P_{41}X_1 + P_{42} X_2 + P_{43} X_3 + P_4 \text{ EXE}$$

Where "P" represents path coefficient, the first subscript or number identifies the dependent variables, the second, dependent variable, "X" represents each variable and "E" represents error terms.

Missing Arrows

Sometimes novice researchers may like to be parsimonious in their path diagram in such a way that an absence of a causal arrow between two variables occurs. A diagram with fewer arrows is generally preferable to one with causal links connecting all variables in both directions, but over-simplicity of theoretical structure can lead to false inferences and erroneous interpretations of research findings. Therefore, causal arrows should be used between variables whenever there is reason to doubt the absence of a causal effect. For instance, the absence of a missing arrow between X_1 and X_3 is illustrated in Figure 3.6:

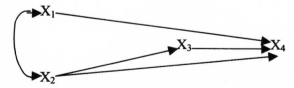

Figure 3.6. Path Diagram with Missing Arrow between X_1 and X_3

According to Heise (1975:13-17), the decision to leave out causal arrow between variables should be justified by the following principles of causal inference: (a) That one event does not directly cause another if no effective operator is available to support the relationship; (b) An event cannot cause another if the first event is not coordinated with existing operators; (c) An event is not caused by other events that occur after it; and (d) If an event A occurs without subsequent occurrence of event B, then A does not cause B in the given circumstances.

Feedback Loops

So far our diagramming of path model on parents' education and children's occupation has been based on unidirectional assumption, *i.e.*, the model is a recursive one in which the causal arrows flow one way. Researchers should understand that the real world might not be a one-way direction because causal feedbacks may defy diagramming in the conventional manner; even feedback loops may be indirect and may not even be explicitly stated in a verbal theory. Feedback loops can be in the form of $X_1 \longleftrightarrow X_2$ or in an indirect form as shown below:

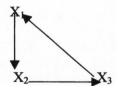

Figure 3.7.   Indirect Feedback Loops

In Figure 3.7 X_2 is dependent on X_1, X_3 is dependent on X_2 and X_1 is dependent on X_3. There is an indirect feedback loop between X_1 and X_2 in that X_1 influences X_2 and X_2 indirectly influences X_1 by going through X_3.

Causal relationships in a path model are specified as unidirectional (recursive) as shown in Figure 3.5 with rare and questionable exceptions (Kerekhoff and Parrow 1979). However, if theory suggests nonrecursiveness among the variables (other than among independent variables themselves) as shown in Figure 3.8 the assumption that the residuals of each regression equation are uncorrelated with the predictors of the equation will be violated. When this happens researchers should employ generalized or two-stage least squares instead of ordinary least squares to compute path coefficients (James and Singh 1978).

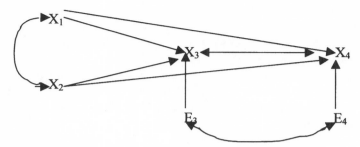

Figure 3.8.   Non-recursive Model with Correlated Error Terms

BENEFITS OF PATH DIAGRAM

Path diagrams provide researchers and theorists with the following advantages stated by Bagozzi (1980:75); Heise (1969:42); Anderson (1973:286); Biddle and Marlin (1987:7); and McClendon (1994): Path diagrams make explicit the assumptions, variables, and hypothesized relationships in one's theory. By clear definition of variables and operationalizations and the functional relationship among variables path diagrams add a certain degree of accuracy to one's theory and research effort. In real life researchers are faced with social and psychological phenomena that involve many complex interactions and feed backs; hence, the path diagram would represents a useful method of understanding such systems of true relationships. They provide a mechanism for constructing and testing the internal adequacy of theories and measurements and also the degree of correspondence between theory and observation.

Whether used to express the causal model or the results of their application, path diagrams are visual representation of a complex argument. They may be lacking in precision when compared to the use of equations, but they are more appealing to the statistically naive readers and authors than the lengthy discussions or the presentation of tabular data. The adoption of path diagrams is clearly one of the reasons for enthusiasm for structural modeling.

LIMITATIONS OF PATH DIAGRAM

In spite of these advantages, path diagrams are associated with the following categories of problems (Biddle and Marlin 1987; Everitt and Dunn 1991). Path diagrams are used for several purposes in structural equation modeling, but there are no agreed upon rules for their use. Different types of path diagrams are used for different purposes. For instance, diagrams of causal models that precede data analysis, of causal models that follow analysis, of models for analysis procedures, of models for analytic findings, and of models that were rejected for some reasons by the users. Unfortunately, no clear rules for constructing these path diagrams exist, and no agreed upon rules for their uses exist either. As a result the unwary reader may find it difficult to sort out the various uses.

Because path model depends upon the researcher's own conception of the causal relationships, misleading path diagrams are sometimes produced since such models cannot be validated or invalidated by analysis.

Researchers usually leave out some important information the readers may need in understanding path diagrams such as the raw correlation from which the regression coefficients were derived, regression coefficients for paths that were not statistically significant, information on significance of differences among regression coefficients, and un-standardized regression coefficients.

Even though path analysis has become popular among researchers, we should remember that no matter how convincing, respectable and reasonable a path diagram may appear any causal inferences made from it is merely a statistical fantasy. Within a given path diagram, path analysis can tell us which paths are important, but it cannot tell us which of the two distinct path diagrams is to be preferred.

SUMMARY

In this chapter, we have discussed the procedure to follow in constructing a path diagram. The importance of theory in constructing a path diagram is clearly stated. The guiding conventions to follow in diagramming causal relationships among variables are explained. The positioning of variables in path diagram and the guiding conventions of such sequence are fully discussed with illustrations. Path symbols that are usually attached with path diagrams are explained with examples. The importance of error terms and feedback loops and the conventions guiding them are fully explained with illustrations. Finally, the benefits and limitations of causal diagrams are also considered. In the next chapter, we will discuss in full the assumptions that must be met before using path analysis.

REFERENCES

Anderson, James G. 1973. "Causal Models and Social Indicators: Toward the Development of Social Systems Models." *American Sociological Review* 38 (3) : 285-301.

Bagozzi, Richard P. 1980. *Causal Models in Marketing*. New York: John Wiley & Sons.

Biddle, Bruce J. and Marjorie M.Marlin. 1987. "Causality, Confirmation, Credulity, and Structural Equation Modeling." *Child Development* 58: 4- 17.

Bohrnstedt, George W. and T. Michael Carter. 1971. "Robustness in Regression Analysis." Pp.118-146 in *Sociological Methodology*, edited by H. L. Costner. San Francisco: Jossey- Bass.

Bohrnstedt, George W. and David Knoke. 1982. *Statistics for Social Data Analysis*. F. E. Peacock Publishers Inc. Itasca. Ill.

Bollen, Kenneth A. and James Scott Long.1993. "Introduction." Pp. 1-9 in *Testing Structural Equation Models*, edited by Kenneth A. Bollen and James Scott Long. Newbury Park, CA: Sage.

Collingwood, R. G. (1940) 1948. *An Essay on Metaphysics*. Oxford: Oxford University Press.

Coser, L. A. 1975. "Presidential Address: Two Methods in Search of a Substance." *American Sociological Review* 40: 691- 700.

Duncan, Otis Dudley. 1971. "Path Analysis: Sociological Examples." Pp. 115-138 in *Causal Models in the Social Sciences*, edited by H. M. Blalock Jr. Chicago: Aldine Publishing Company.

Everitt, B. S. and G. Dunn. 1991. *Applied Multivariate Data Analysis*. New York: Halsted Press. Pp.257-275.

Gujarati, Damodar. 1978. *Basic Econometrics*. New York: McGraw Hill.

Hanson, N. R.1958. *Pattern of Discovery*. Cambridge: Cambridge University Press.

Heise, David R. 1969. "Problems in Path Analysis and Causal Inferences." Pp. 38-73 in *Sociological Methodology*, edited by E. F. Borgatta and G. W. Bohrnstedt. San Francisco: Jossey- Bass.

———. 1975. *Causal Analysis*. New York: John Wiley & Sons, Inc.

Hetherington, John. 2000. "Role of Theory and Experimental Design in Multivariate Analysis and Mathematical Modeling." Pp. 37 - 63 in *Handbook of Applied Multivariate Statistics and Mathematical Modeling,* edited by Howard E. A Tinsley and Stephen D. Brown. San Diego, CA: Academic Press.

Holland, P. W. 1986. "Statistics and Causal Inferences (with discussion)." *Journal of The American Statistical Association* 81: 945 –970.

James, Lawrence R. and K. Singh. 1978. "An Introduction to The Logic, Assumptions, and Basic Analytic Procedures of Two-stage Least Squares." *Psychological Bulletin* 85: 1104 – 1122.

Joreskog, K. G. and M. Van Thillo. 1972. *LISTREL: A General Computer Program for Estimating a Linear Structural Equation System Involving Multiple Indicators of Unmeasured Variables*. Educational Testing Service. Princeton, N J: Research Bulletin # 72-56.

Kerckhoff, A. C. and A. C. Parrows. 1979. "The Effect of Early Marriage on The Educational Attainment of Young Men." *Journal of Marriage and The Family* 41: (February): 97-107.

Kmenta, Jan. 1971. *Elements of Econometrics*. New York: Macmillan Publishing Company.

Land, Kenneth C. 1969. "Principles of Path Analysis." Pp.3- 37 in *Sociological Methodology,* edited by E. F. Borgotta and G. W. Bohrnstedt. San Francisco: Jossey-Bass.

MacCallum, Robert C. 1995. "Model Specification: Procedures, Strategies, and Related Issues." Pp. 16-36 in *Structural Equation Modeling: Concepts, Issues, and Application* edited by Rick H. Hoyle. Thousand Oaks, CA: Sage Publication

MacDonald, K. I. 1977. "Path Analysis." Pp. 81-104 in *The Analysis of Survey Data.* Vol. 2, edited by G. A. O' Muircheartaigh and C. Payne. New York: Wiley & Sons.

Maxim, Paul S. 1999. *Quantitative Research Methods in The Social Sciences.* New York: Oxford University Press.

McClendon, McKee J. 1994. *Multiple Regression and Causal Analysis.* Itasca, IL: Peacock Publishers.

Pedhazur, Elazar J. 1982. *Multiple Regressions in Behavioral Research: Explanation and Prediction.* New York: Holt, Rinehart, and Winston.

Sobel, Michael E. 1990. "Effects Analysis and Causation in Linear Structural Equation Models." *Psychometrika* 55: 495-515.

Chapter Four

Assumptions

After constructing path diagram, the next step is to consider the conditions (assumptions) under which path analysis can be applied. Assumptions are the set of rules under which a statistical technique is carried out. Before using any statistical technique researchers must strive to satisfy all of the assumptions underlying it for the following reasons: (a) The validity of the technique used in analyzing data depends on whether certain assumptions underlying it are satisfied; (b) Because statistical technique may not work well in all situations, assumptions guide the researcher by specifying the conditions under which the technique may work well (Allison 1999:119), and (c) Failure to meet the assumptions may render our findings and conclusions meaningless and erroneous (Champion 1970), *i.e.*, the technique we use may seem to tell us more of what we want to know than our data can possibly provide (Mosteller and Turkey 1977: 320). In practice, of course, we do not insist on absolute adherence to the basic assumptions because of their robustness (Bohrnstedt and Carter 1971) but are satisfied when these assumptions hold only approximately (Kmenta 1986: 209).

In path analysis, many assumptions deal with the relationship between variables that guide researchers in building causal models and hypothesis testing. The relationship between variables in a causal model is a linear relationship in which a change in one variable always occurs as a linear function of change in another variable. Y is a linear function of X: $Y = \beta X$. That is the causal effect is a linear effect.

For a better understanding of linearity in causal effect it is appropriate to distinguish between linearity in the variables and linearity in the parameters. According to Guajarati (1978:24) and Chatterjee and Price (1991:32), linearity in the variables is the "natural" meaning of linearity that the conditional expectation of Y is a linear function of Xi such as $E(Y/Xi) = \beta o + \beta 1 X 1$.

That is, the dependent variable (Y) and independent variable (X) are arranged to fit a line to the plot of data that shows a straight-line relationship between the variables as indicated in this diagram:

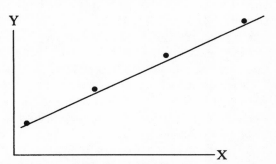

Figure 4.1.   Linearity in the variables of Hypothetical Data

But linearity in the parameters is the conditional expectation of Y, $E(Y/Xi)$, is a linear function of the parameters, the β's; it may or may not be linear in variable X. A function is said to be linear in the parameter, if β_1 appears with a power of 1 only and is not multiplied or divided by any other parameter (*i.e.*, $\beta o \beta_1$, β_1/β_1, and so on). A regression model is linear when the parameters present in the model occur linearly. That is a change in one variable (X) causes a change in another variable (Y). Therefore, in discussing the term "linearity" in causal models and structural equation systems we mean linearity in parameters because linearity in the parameters is relevant for the development of the regression theory and it is the most violated assumption.

Linear relationship is mostly in Cartesian coordinate in equation form:

$$Y = \alpha + \beta x$$

Where α is the intercept parameter and the slope parameter β. In the process of inquiry it may be very impossible to include all necessary variables due to some uncertainties and those variables excluded are represented by the term, "μ," which reflects the error terms or disturbances. That is a linear regression model is in equation form:

$$Y = \alpha + \beta X + \mu$$

The relationship between independent and dependent variables in a causal model is parallel to that in a linear regression model, and path analysis is essentially an extension and specific application of multiple regressions. Therefore, the assumptions of linear regression model can be applied to causal relationship for the following reasons: (a) Linear model presents a reasonable assumption which can be useful in testing hypothesis in path analysis and in building a path model; (b) Linear function fits the empirical data in path analysis because linear processes fundamentally govern most relationships in the world. For example, many psychological and social phenomena are linear and many theoretical statements in the social sciences can be reasonably modeled as such (Dawes and Corrigan 1974; Allen 1997); (c) Since linear regression models only require that there be linearity in the expected value of known functions of the explanatory variables, it is often possible to represent more complex processes (like path analysis) using the linear model (Bagozzi 1980: 70), because linear functions are less complex than most other mathematical functions, and the principle of parsimony suggests that we should choose simple explanations over more complex ones(Allen 1997); and (d) Since the same statistical technique (i.e. ordinary least squares) is used to estimate parameters in both regression and path analysis, many of the basic assumptions of each method are identical (Schumm et. al.1980: 252).

For appropriate application of the assumptions users/researchers using path analysis should be familiar with the basic assumptions as discussed under the following subheadings:

1. Explicit statement of the assumptions.

2. The rationale for such assumptions.

3. Testing the assumptions to detect possible violations can be done through any of the following methods: (a) By using theoretical considerations or examining how data were measured; (b) By looking at the type of data used and how they were collected. For example, equations estimated from time series data are frequently characterized by auto-correlated disturbances, while those from survey data can be heteroskedastic; (c) By plotting the least squares residuals against either the sample values of independent variable (X), or the fitted values of dependent variable ($\hat{Y}$). No violation of assumptions exists if the residual plots show no distinct pattern of variation. (For SPSS program to test assumptions, see Mertler & Vannatta 2001:Chapters 3&7). Interpretation of plot is based on subjective judgment and requires skill and experience; and (d) By using statistical techniques.

4. The consequences of violations should be stated.

5. Dealing with violations.

LINEARITY AND ADDITIVITY

In linearity, it is assumed that the conditional expectation of Y, E (Y/Xi), is a linear function of the parameters, the β's; it may or may not be linear in the variable X. That is, the regression model is linear when the parameters present in the model occur linearly. In a linear relationships, it is assumed that for each independent variable Xi, the amount of change in the mean value of Y associated with a unit change in Xi, holding all other independent variables constant, is the same regardless of the value of Xi (Heise 1969; Bohrnstedt and Carter 1971; Lewis-Beck 1980; Asher 1976; Schumm et al. 1980; Chatterjee and Price 1977; Berry and Feldman 1985; Jobson 1991).

The linearity requirement eliminates multiplicative or interaction relations like $X = y^2$; exponential relationships like $y = 2^X$; and curvilinear relationships like $y = X^3$ (Heise 1969:45). Linearity can be stated in equation form as follows:

$$Y = \alpha + b_1X_1 + b_2X_22 + b_3X_3 \ldots b_nX_n + e$$

Or

$$Yi = \alpha + \beta Xi + ei$$

Where Y is called the "dependent variable," X the "independent variable," and e the "stochastic disturbance," α and β are the "regression parameters" which are unknown, the subscript "i" refers to the ith observations. Linearity can be positive or negative. Positive linearity shows that as the magnitude of X (independent variable) increases the magnitude of Y (dependent variable) constantly increases in a specified amount. Negative linearity means that as the magnitude of X decreases the magnitude of Y constantly increases in a specified amount. Both positive and negative linearity can be shown thus:

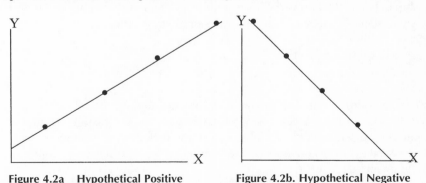

Figure 4.2a Hypothetical Positive Linearity

Figure 4.2b. Hypothetical Negative Linearity

Additivity assumption states that for each independent variable Xi the amount of change in E (Y) associated with a unit increase in Xi (holding all independent variables constant) is the same regardless of the values of the other independent variables in the equation (Berry and Feldman 1985).

Rationale

The theoretical reasoning for this assumption is to explain the variation of Y in terms of the variation in the variable X, assumed to be linearly related to Y in order to maximize accuracy and minimize error in prediction.

Testing for Linearity and Additivity

Linearity and additivity can be tested for by using any of the following techniques:

1. The first step in detecting non-linearity and non-additivity is to use theory underlying the model to determine the hypothesized form of non-linearity or non-additivity (Berry and Feldman 1985:53). Once the nature of the expected non-linearity and non-additivity is well understood to make a rough graph of its form, use the methods stated by Berry and Feldman (1985); Kmenta (1986); Lahiri and Egy (1981); Allison (1999); Jobson (1991); Gujarati (1978); Utts (1982); Spitzer (1984) to detect them:

2. Examine the scatter diagram of the sample relationship between the independent and dependent variables. If the points on the graph do not take the form of a line it means the relationship is not linear.

3. Divide the cases into several sub samples each of which includes a range of values for the independent variable. If regression slope and intercept estimates generated differ substantially across sub samples, it means the relationship between the two variables is nonlinear. The F- test can be used to test any significant differences from one sub sample to another.

$$F = \frac{(R^2 - R^2m)/r}{(1 - R^2)/(n - k - r - 1)}$$

For non additivity, divide the samples into sub samples based on the values of the cases for the independent variables, then run regression on a model containing the independent variable and terms including dichotomous variables. Use the F-test above to test for any significant differences from one sample to another.

4. Use the Power Function Test. The basic idea of this test is that a linear function is a special case of a power function of degree one. If the coefficients attached to the higher powers of the explanatory variables are all zero, the given power function reduces to a simple linear regression.

5. Linearity can be detected by using Box-Cox transformation.

6. Linearity can be also detected by using The Likelihood Ratio Test:

$$LR = -2[L\ (\lambda=1) - L(\hat{\lambda})] \sim X_1^2$$

7. When the regression equation is linear but heteroskedastic, a joint test (of the likelihood ratio type) for linearity and homoskedasticity or for linearity and non-autocorrelation is applicable or preferable.

8. Another method is to fit a quadratic function to the data.

9. The P E Test can be used when the only alternative to linear regression is log linear regression.

10. Use the scatter plot of the residual to test whether the disturbances are normally scattered around the population regression line. If the population regression is not linear, the scatter of the disturbances around a straight line will no longer be random.

11. Graph the estimated regression equation.

12. We can also use the Durbin Watson Test.

13. When replicated data are not available the "Rainbow" test can be used as an alternative.

Effects of Violation

If this assumption is not met, it means observations are not arranged linearly along the regression line and parameter estimates may be severely biased (Land 1969; Asher 1976). This may affect our beta weight because we would not be able to know how much a standardized unit change in X causes in Y. Hence, it may be difficult to predict from our data.

Dealing with Non linearity and Additivity

When this assumption is violated, the variables can still be used because some techniques are available to offset the effects of such violation. (Heise 1969, Bohrnstedt and Carter1971). The problem of non-linearity and non-additivity can be removed by using any of the following techniques (Berry and Feldman 1985; Lewis-Beck 1977; Friedrich 1982; Allison 1999):

For non-linearity use any of the following techniques:

1. Transform the dependent variable by taking logarithm and logit transformation.

2. Use polynomial models to transform the independent variables.

3. Use the exponential model.

4. Use the hyperbolic model.

For non-additivity use any of the following techniques:

1. Use the dummy variable interactive model.

2. Use a single-equation model including the dummy variable as an independent variable.

3. Use the multiplicative model.

4. Use a nonlinear interactive model.

INTERVAL LEVEL MEASUREMENT

Path analysis assumes that the variables used are either interval or ratio level measurement (Heise 1969; Land 1969; Berry and Feldman 1985; Bohrnstedt and Carter 1971). That is, the data are of equal distance measurement so that it is possible to specify the exact numbers. Interval level data make it possible to do subtraction, addition, and multiplication because there is a zero point. Using variables measured at the ordinal and categorical levels violates this assumption. Logit, probit, or discriminant analysis are appropriate estimation procedures when dependent variables are measured at the ordinal or categorical level (Hanushek and Jackson 1977: Chapter: 7; Klecka 1979; Aldrich and Nelson 1984).

Rationale

The reasoning for this assumption is to provide enough precision to distinguish simple linear relationships and more complex relationship shapes, such as quadratic or logarithmic patterns. Such precision is essential in a research that attempts to verify theoretical models containing more complicated relationships (Schumm et al. 1980: 254).

Testing for Interval Level of Measurement

Observe the level of measurement of each variable.

Effects of Violation

To some investigators like Stevens (1959), Wilson (1971), and Wolinksky et al. (1976), violation of this assumption will make the result of a research in which such data are used inconclusive no matter what kind of transformation is applied to remedy the data, because transformation of ordinal data into interval level data will reverse its conclusion. To others, variables measured at the ordinal level can be used (Boyle 1970; Bohrnstedt and Carter 1971; Lyons

1971; Asher 1976) especially when as many rankings as possible are obtained (Labovitz 1970).

Dealing with Non interval Level

Despite the violations, variables measured at the ordinal level can be used because there is monotonic relationship between the underlying continuum and the ordinal scale, hence the application of a test of significance to ordinal data yields few abberations (Labovitz 1967, 1970; Baker et al. 1966; Burke 1953; Borgatta 1968,1970; Bohrnstedt and Carter 1971; Jacobson 1970; Boyle 1970; Lyon and Carter 1971).

MEASUREMENT ERROR

This assumption states that independent variables are measured without error in order to assure unbiased parameter estimate (Heise 1969; Kmenta 1971; Bohrnstedt and Carter 1971; Johnston 1972), parameter variances (Block 1978) and un-attenuated multiple R^2s (Cochran 1970). It is also assumed that the values of independent variables are fixed or selected in advance (Chatterjee and Price 1977, 1991). (For a full discussion on measurement error see Carmines and Zeller 1979)

Rationale

The reasoning behind this assumption is to see that our concepts are precisely defined and our measuring instruments are accurate so that our variables may be highly reliable.

Testing for Measurement Error

Measurement error can be detected by any of the following procedures and the type of data will determine the appropriate procedure to use. The appropriate time to detect the presence of measurement error is before a regression equation is estimated.

1. Measurement error can be detected by assessing the empirical measurement through any of the following reliability methods: Test-retest method, alternative-form method, split halves method, and internal consistency method (Bohrnstedt 1970; Carmines and Zeller 1979; Nunnally 1964; Stanley 1971; Cronbach 1951; Novick and Lewis 1967).

2. Multiple indicators of variables can be used to detect measurement error (Sullivan and Feldman 1979).

3. Estimating the bounds for the true regression coefficients can assess measurement error in the explanatory variable. This involves obtaining least squares estimates by regressing Y* on X* and conversely X* on Y*. The width of the interval given by the two sets of estimates gives an indication of the seriousness of the presence of measurement error for estimation (Kmenta 1986).

4. Measurement error can also be detected by using instrumental variable estimates and their estimated standard errors to construct confidence intervals for the true regression coefficients. There is measurement error if the ordinary least square estimates fall outside of the respective intervals (Sargan 1958).

5. Hausman Test can also be used to detect measurement error in the explanatory variable (Hausman 1978; Kmenta 1986).

Effects of Violation

Violation of this assumption will make the empirically observed slope, b, which is used as an estimation of p, less than the true slope and therefore give wrong estimates for path coefficients (Heise 1969:58). Existence of measurement error will make the disturbance terms correlate with the independent variables and with themselves and therefore lead to biased estimates of the path coefficients. (Bohrnstedt and Carter 1971). Measurement error in the independent variable may lead to an upward or downward bias in the estimation of the regression coefficients and also severely distorts the interpretation of the relative sizes of different regression coefficients (Cochran 1968; Berry and Feldman 1985).

Dealing with Measurement Error

Despite these effects of violation, variables with measurement error can still be used with no serious effects on the estimates of the ordinary least squares parameter because it is assumed that the independent variables may not correlate with the error terms or disturbances in the model (Kmenta 1971; Johnston 1972) and the error can be removed by any of the following methods:

1. Data collection and coding methods should be designed to minimize the intrusion of random errors. Multiple indicators of a concept should be collected in obtaining estimates of measurement error and constructing scales

with reliable measures (Berry and Feldman 1985; McIver and Carmines 1981).

2. Instrumental variable can be used to derive an estimate of partial slope coefficient βi for the variable Xi purged of the random error component that is biasing the estimate and the estimate of partial regression coefficients that are unbiased in large samples (Berry and Feldman 1985; McAdams 1984).

3. Use multiple indicator models when there are multiple measures of the variables in the analysis to produce estimates of the coefficients of the model free from the effect of measurement error and also deal with both random and nonrandom measurement error (Kmenta 1986). See Sullivan and Feldman (1979) for the logic, and Long (1983) for an introduction to such models.

HOMOSKEDASTICITY

It is assumed in homoskedasticity that the error terms are randomly distributed across values of each independent variable (Heise 1969: Gujarati 1978; Chatterjee and Price 1977, 1991; Kmenta 1986; Bohrnstedt and Carter 1971). Heteroskedasticity, (lack of homoskedasticity) occurs when the error terms are not equally distributed across values of each independent variable. Heteroskedasticity is expressed in equation form by Gujarati (1978:39) thus:

$$\text{Var } (\mu i / Xi) = \delta i^2$$

where the subscript on δ^2 indicates that the variance of X population is no longer constant. For graphical illustrations, see Gujarati (1978); Chatterjee and Price (1977, 1991); and Allison (1999); Kelejian and Oates (1974); and Draper and Smith (1966).

Heteroskedasticity can occur under the following conditions stated by Berry and Feldman (1985): (a) If the dependent variable is measured with error, and the amount of error varies with the value of independent variable; (b) If the unit of analysis is an "aggregate" and the dependent variable is an average of values for the individual objects composing the aggregate units; and (c), there is substantively meaningful variation in the independent variable.

Rationale

The reasoning for this assumption is that all observations would be equally reliable if the variance of error terms (μ) were the same for all observations. (Kelejian and Oates 1974: 39)

Testing for Heteroskedasticity

The presence of heteroskedasticity can be detected by any of the following procedures:

1. Examine the scatter diagram in which regression residuals are plotted against the independent variable. There is heteroskedasticity if the variances of residuals increase as X increases (Berry and Feldman 1985; Rao and Miller 1971; Chatterjee and Price 1977, 1991; Jobson 1991; McClendon 1994).

2. Use Glejser Test by regressing the absolute values of regression residuals for the sample in the values of the independent variable thought to co-vary with the variance of the error term (Berry and Feldman 1985; Glejser 1969).

3. Use the Goldfeld and Quandt Test. The idea is that if sample observations are generated under the conditions of homoskedasticity, then the variance of the disturbances is the same in all parts of the sample observations (Berry and Feldman 1985; Kmenta 1986).

4. Use the White Test to compare the sample variance of the least squares estimators under homoskedasticity and heteroskedasticity. When there is homoskedasticity, the two estimated variances would, in large samples, differ only because of sampling fluctuation (Kmenta 1986; McClendon 1994).

5. Use the Bartlett Test (generically known as "Likelihood ratio test") when there are several observations on the dependent variable for each different value of the explanatory variable. There is heteroskedasticity if the values of the maximized likelihood function obtained for homoskedasticity differ greatly from that obtained for possible heteroskedasticity (Kmenta 1986).

6. Use the Breusch-Pagan Test (generically known as "Lagrange multiplier test"). No significant difference between the ordinary least squares estimates of the regression coefficients and the maximum likelihood estimates for possible heteroskedasticity indicates that the hypothesis of homoskedasticity is true (Kmenta 1986).

7. When dealing with time series observations we may wish to test the hypothesis of homoskedasticity against the alternative of auto regressive conditional heteroskedasticity (ARCH). The appropriate test developed by Engle involves using squared least squares residuals and applying the least squares method to

$$e^2_t = \lambda_0 + \lambda_1 e^2_{t-1} + \lambda_2 e^2_{t-2} + \ldots + \lambda_p e^2_{t-p} + u_t$$

(Kmenta 1986; Engle 1982).

8. The presence of heteroskedasticity can also be detected by transformation of regression equation so that the transformed disturbance becomes homoskedastic leads to a nonlinear form of transformed regression equation.

Effects of Violation

When heteroskedasticity occurs, significance tests will have low sensitivity and substantially large path coefficients may be rejected as statistically insignificant (Schumm et al. 1980; Lewis-Beck 1980; Gujarat 1978; Berry and Feldman 1985). If ordinary least squares is applied to the raw data, the resulting estimated coefficient will lack precision in a theoretical sense and the estimated standard errors of regression coefficients are understated, giving a false sense of precision (Chatterjee and Price 1977:102; Jobson 1991).

Dealing with Heteroskedasticity

Despite the effects, violation of this assumption may not have serious effect on the result of the study or the number of significant F-tests and their magnitude unless heterogeneity among the variance is marked (Bohrnstedt and Carter 1971; Cochran 1947; Berry and Feldman 1985). The problem can be solved by any of the following methods:

1. If the presence of heteroskedasticity is a result of an interaction of an independent variable with some variables not included in the model, we must use sound theory to suggest potential variables to be included or excluded. Use weighted least squares to eliminate heteroskedasticity. This is equivalent to a special transformation applied to both Y and X before determining the ordinary least squares fit (Judge et al. 1985; Jobson 1991:168; Berry and Feldman 1985).

2. If heteroskedasticity is a result of the nature of measurement of dependent variable, an aggregated unit of analysis, or other problems, the analyst is free to assume that OLS estimators are unbiased but not BLUE and can use generalized least square (GLS) to yield estimators that are BLUE (Wonnacott and Wonnacott 1979: Chapter:16; Hanushek and Jackson 1977).

3. When heteroskedasticity is present and conforms to one of a few specific "functional forms," weighted least squares (WLS) procedures utilizing OLS regression or a transformed version of the regression model can be used on the assumption that the standard deviation of the error term is linearly related to one of the independent variables (Berry and Feldman 1985: 87; Kmenta 1986; Jobson 1991:168).

4. Another method to reduce heteroskedasticity is to transform the dependent variable by using variance-stabilizing transformation (Mendenhall & Sincich 1996). The problem with this method is that it changes the nature of the relationship between the dependent and independent variables and makes the coefficients more difficult to interpret.

LACK OF AUTO CORRELATION

This assumption states that the residuals (error terms) are not correlated with each other (Schumm et al. 1980; Chatterjee and Price 1991; Kmenta 1986; Lewis- Beck 1980; Asher 1976). It implies that the disturbance occurring at one point of observation is not correlated with any other disturbance. This assumption is expressed in equation form by Gujarati (1978:37): Cov (μi, μj) = O $i \neq j$. This means that error terms should be independent of one another so that one cannot determine one error term from the other, *i.e.*, there is no auto correlation. When error terms are correlated (auto correlation) it means that this assumption is violated. Error terms can correlate positively or negatively when there is autocorrelation. For graphical illustrations, see Gujarati (1978:38).

The following situations stated by Chatterjee and Price (1991); Berry and Feldman (1985); and Allison (1999) may lead to the presence of autocorrelation:

1. When adjacent residuals are similar in both temporal and spatial dimensions.

2. Successive residuals in economic time series are positively correlated.

3. Large positive errors are followed by other negative errors.

4. When observations sampled under similar condition from adjacent experimental plots or area tend to residuals that are correlated.

5. If the values of relevant variables omitted in the regression equation are correlated, the errors from the estimated model will appear to be correlated.

6. If two individuals have one of the unmeasured variables in common.

7. If the behavior of one person affects the behavior of another person in the same sample.

8. When the same individuals are measured at multiple points in time.

9. Error terms will correlate with one another if the data are not collected through simple random sampling.

Rationale

The reasoning for this assumption is to specify a model with one predictable force (X) affecting the dependent variable. This would not be possible if the disturbance terms were related to each other (Kelejian and Oates 1974: 40).

Testing for Auto correlation

The presence of auto correlation can be detected by any of the following tests.

1. The Geary Test. This test involves counting of sign changes in the regression residuals to determine whether there is positive or negative auto cor-

relation. Few sign changes means positive serial correlation and large number of sign changes means negative serial correlation (Habibagahi and Pratschke 1972:184; Ostrom1978: 32).

2. Use the Durbin-Watson d-Statistics (Kmenta 1986; Ostrom 1978; Chatterjee and Price 1977;Gujarati 1978; Kelejian and Oates 1974; Jobson 1991).

3. Examine the scatter plot of the residuals plotted against the independent variables (Gujarati 1978; Jobson 1991).

4. Transform the data.

5. Use the Theil-Nagar Q-Values (Theil and Nagar1961; Ostrom1978).

6. Hildreth-Lu method can be used (Ostrom 1978: 39; Kmenta 1971: 282-287).

7. The Cochrane-Orcutt procedure can be used to detect auto correlation (Jobson 1991; Kmenta 1986).

8. First Differences method can be used (Ostrom 1978: 40; Kmenta 1971, 1986).

9. The M-Test is another technique for detecting auto correlation (Kmenta 1986: 333).

10. Use the Runs Tests that can be used for any nonrandom pattern (Ostle and Mensing, 1975).

Effects of Violation

The effects of violating this assumption are well stated by Chatterjee and Price (1991); Gujarati (1978); Ostrom (1978); Jobson (1991); Freund and Wilson (1998) as follow: (a) Least square estimates (a, b) are unbiased but not efficient in that they no longer have property of being the best linear unbiased estimators; (b) Estimation of variance (σ^2) and standard error of the regression coefficient may be seriously understated. That is, the estimated standard error will be much smaller than they actually are, hence giving a spurious impression of accuracy; (c) Confidence intervals and tests of significance (t and F) will not be valid; and (d) Violation can have an important impact on the quality of the inferences we draw from our empirical analysis.

Dealing with Auto correlation

The problem of auto correlation can be solved by any of the following methods:

1 Include the relevant variables excluded. That is, use a simple redefinition of the model (also a transformation) (Fuller 1996).

2. Use transformation to incorporate estimates of the auto-correlation coefficients (Freund and Wilson 1998:168; Jobson 1991).

3. If there is no indication of significant serial auto correlation, we can accept the OLS estimates without fearing a loss of efficiency or bias in estimated variance.

4. Use estimation technique if there is significant auto correlation. If the effects are serious, one can adopt Theil and Nagar's Q-Test or Durbin –Watson's test and take corrective action (Fomby, Hill and Johnson 1984; Judge, et al. 1985).

5. Use Generalized Least Square (GLS), a technique that will always yield estimators that are BLUE when auto correlation is present (Ostrom 1978; Hibbs 1974; Green 1997).

LACK OF MULTICOLLINEARITY

This assumption states that none of the independent variables is perfectly correlated with any other independent variable or with any linear combination of other independent variables. The concern about multicollinearity is much less between its presence and absence than between its various degrees.

Conditions for Multicollinearity

Multicollinearity can be caused by the following factors (Allison 1999; Jobson 1991; Chatterjee and Price 1991)

1. The sample may in some way be artificially restricted.

2. It can occur because of some artifact in the way the independent variables are constructed.

3. Multicollinearity may also be natural to the population and can only be eliminated by model re-specification.

4. It can also be a result of too few observations for too many variables.

5. Multicolinearity can result from deficient sample data and/or inter-relationships among the variables used in our investigation.

6. Data collected in time series design are likely to have variables that are highly correlated because of the consistent long term trends in many different variables.

7. Multicollinearity is common in panel study in that many cases are observed at two or more points in time.

8. Aggregated, group level or categorical data may also contribute to multicollinearity because random variation among individual people tends to average out in groups.

Rationale

The rationale for this assumption is that if there is perfect multicollinearity the regression coefficients of the independent variables are indeterminate and their standard errors are infinite. However if less than perfect, the regression coefficients, although determinate, possess large standard errors and cannot be estimated with great precision or accuracy (Gujarati 1978: 173).

Testing for Multicollinearity

Multicollinearity refers to the condition of the explanatory variables that are assumed to be non stochastic therefore, it is a feature of the sample and not of the population. The concern is not whether it exists, but about the degree and there are no tests to provide irrefutable information about whether multicollinearity is, or is not a problem (Berry and Feldman 1985:42). Several warning signals exist to determine the degree of multicollinearity such as the following:

1. By examining the stability of coefficient estimates across different samples, or slightly different specifications of a model using the same model. There is high multicollinearity when switching samples, changing the indicators used to measure a variable in the regression model, or deleting or adding a variable to the equation can lead to large changes in the size of coefficients (Chatterjee and Price 1977;Berry and Feldman 1985).

2. There is multicollinearity if the algebraic signs of the estimated coefficients do not conform to prior expectations.

3. Multicollinearity should be suspected when none of the t-ratios for the regression coefficients for independent variables is sufficiently large to indicate statistical significance at the .05 percent level, yet the F-statistics for the full model is significant (Berry and Feldman 1985).

4. The eigen-value structure of R can be used to detect the presence of multicollinearity (Jobson 1991:281).

5. The ratio $K = \lambda i/\lambda p$ commonly called multicollinearity condition number can be used to detect multicollinearity. There is multicollinearity if the condition number is less than 100 (Jobson 1991: 281-282; Berk 1977).

6. The matrix of eigenvectors V derived from R^{-1} can also be used to detect the sources of multicollinearity by examining the variances of the estimated regression coefficients (Jobson 1991).

7. Multicolinearity can also be detected by including the intercept in the condition number (Jobson 1991: 282-284; Belsey 1984).

8. Use latent root regression (Jobson 1991:290).

9. There is multicollinearity if coefficients of variables that are expected to be important have large standard errors.

10. There is problem of multicollinearity if the matrix or bivariate correlations show correlation exceeding •80 (Kmenta 1986; Jobson 1991).

11. There is a high degree of multicollinearity if R^2 between the two independent variables is close to 1.00 (Lemieux 1978; Chatterjee and Pice 1991; Kmenta 1986; Jobson 1991).

12. By using the Principal Components of the explanatory set of variables (Chatterjee and Price 1991:193; Jobson 1991; Press 1972).

13. By using Ridge regression analysis (Hoerl and Kennard 1970; Chatterjee and Price 1991; Jobson 1991).

14. Variance Inflation Factors or variance proportions can also be used to detect multicollinearity (Freund and Wilson 1998).

Effects of Violation

Before examining the effects of multicollinearity, the following points should be taken into account (Berry and Feldman 1985:38): (a) Multicollinearity refers to correlation among independent variables in a specific sample of data, rather than data collected through controlled experiments; (b) the presence of high multicollinearity does not violate the assumption of regression in that OLS slope coefficient estimators remain BLUE; and (c) the concern about multicollinearity is not whether it exists or not, but about its magnitude. Therefore, the effect is not serious when the magnitude is small, but becomes more serious as the magnitude increases.

Despite these points the effects of violation are still important for the following reasons discussed by Asher (1976); Schumm et al. (1980); Gujarati (1978); Lewis-Beck (1980); Allison (1999); Freund and Wilson (1998); Berry and Feldman (1985):

1. Path coefficients will display opposite signs than those found in zero- order correlation.

2. The standard errors of ordinary least square estimators tend to be large as the degree of collinearity between variables increases.

3. Due to large standard errors, the confidence intervals for coefficients tend to be very wide, and t-statistics for significance tests tend to be very small.

4. The partial slope coefficients are affected in that it is impossible to isolate the individual effects of the explanatory variables.

5. Coefficients are less robust because multicollinearity makes multiple regression much more sensitive to minor errors.

6. Multicollinearity makes regression analysis less effective in determining the effects of the various independent factor variables.

7. The model with all variables may not fit the data than models with fewer variables.

Dealing with Multicollinearity

The problem of multicolinearity can be reduced by any of the following methods:

1. According to Kmenta (1986) and Allison (1999), the best solution to multicollinearity is by collecting better data as follows: (a) Increasing the sample size will reduce the inflated standard errors that stem from multi-collinearity; (b) Use individual level data instead of aggregate data; (c) Use cross sectional data instead of time series data; (d) Use stratified sampling on the independent variables.

2. Perform joint hypothesis tests.

3. If no other observations are available use prior knowledge about the values of the regression coefficients themselves (Berry and Feldman 1985).

4. Identify and estimate informative linear functions of the regression coefficients.

5. Transform the model.

6. Use variable selection methods (Freund and Wilson 1998: Chapter 6).

7. Use information about the known relationships to redefine the independent variables in the model.

8. Create a new set of independent variables by using the results of Principal Components (Freund & Wilson 1998).

9. Combine highly correlated independent variables into a single variable. This approach is only appropriate when the variables combined into a composite are multiple indicators of the same underlying theoretical concepts (Carmines and Zeller 1979; Jobson 1991; Allison 1999). When correlated variables are multiple indicators of the same concept, we can re-specify the model in the form of a multiple indicator model, and estimate coefficients using path analytic procedures (Sullivan and Feldman 1979) or a maximum- likelihood approach such as LISTREL (Long 1983; Jobson 1991).

10. Use biased estimation methods such as incomplete principal component regression and the ridge regression (Freund and Wilson 1998).

11. Dropping one or more principal components from the regression on a theoretical basis can also eliminate multicollinearity. This is equivalent to imposing constraints on the regression coefficients. (That is, delete from the equation the variable that is causing the problem). Because this method can yield biased estimators of the coefficients for the included variable, other estimation methods may be preferred if the model is to be used for other purposes than prediction.

12. We may acknowledge the presence of multicollinearity and live with its consequences (Chatterjee and Price 1977; Berry and Feldman 1985).

NORMALITY

The assumption of normality states that the residuals are normally distributed with a mean of zero, as a basis for the use of parametric tests of statistical significance (Berry and Feldman 1985; Land 1969; Kmenta 1986; Asher 1976). Therefore, over 95% of the residuals should fall within two standard deviations of either side of their mean.

Rationale

Some of the reasoning for this assumption expressed by Gujarati (1978: 72); Mood (1950.142-143), and Kmenta (1986:97) are the following: (a) According to the central limit theorem the shape of the sampling distribution of the mean will approximate a normal distribution if the sample size is sufficiently large. (b) Another reasoning for this assumption is that if a complete theory of statistical inference is developed based on the normal distribution alone, then, one has in reality a system that may be employed quite generally, because other distributions can be transformed to the normal form. (c) If it is assumed that all small errors are equal and that both positive and negative deviations are likely; then it can be shown that the errors are normally distributed about zero, i.e. the measurements are normally distributed about the true value. (d) Normality is needed to prove the efficiency of the least squares estimators of the regression coefficients by means of the Cramer-Rao lower bound, and also to establish confidence intervals and tests of significance.

Testing for Normality

Violation of this assumption can be detected by any of the following tests (Kmenta 1986; Jobson 1991; Hoaglin, Mosteller and Turkey 1985; Huber 1981; Johnson and Wichern 1982):

1. Examine the scatter plot of residuals against independent variables.

2. Calculate both Least Squares (LS) and Minimizing the sum of Absolute Deviation (MAD) estimates of the regression coefficients to determine if they are not too far apart. If there is a substantial difference between them, identify those observations with extreme deviations and check their cause, including the possibility of gross error of measurement or recording.

3. Calculate the residuals from the regression and see if they follow something like a normal distribution.

4. Test for the values of the moments corresponding to the shape of distribution in question. This is a natural way to test for a particular shape of a distribution

5. Use the Kolmogorov- Smirnov (K-S) Test to compare the observed cumulative probability function and a hypothesized theoretical cumulative probability function.

6. Use the P-P Plot (Probability -Probability Plot). In this test, the sample cumulative probability distribution S(x) is compared to the theoretical cumulative probability function F(x) for a set of common X values. The data is normally distributed if the observations are on a straight line with intercept O and slope 1. If the observations are not normal-like, the plot will be nonlinear.

7. Use The Q-Q Plot (The Quantile-Quantile Plot) to compare the observed quantiles to the theoretical quantiles. The plot will be a straight line through the origin with slope 1 if the data are normally distributed and the distribution of the data is non-normal if the plot is nonlinear.

8. Use The Residuals Plot to check normality by plotting the studentized residual on the vertical axis against either the predicted values $\hat{Y}$ or the explanatory variable X on the horizontal axis. Departure from normality is not usually serious if the distribution of the residuals is bell-shaped without outliers.

9. The Wilk-Shapiro or W-Test may be used to compare the conventional estimator of the variance to an estimator of variance that employs the order statistics under the assumption of normality.

10. Another test is based on the property that $\bar{x}$ and s^2 are independent if the underlying population is normal.

11. Test of the null hypothesis can be used to test normality assumption:

Ho: $B_1 = 0$ and $B_2 = 3$

For details on testing null hypothesis see Kmenta 1986: 267.

Effects of Violation

Violation of this assumption is not a serious matter because normality assumption can be relaxed for large samples due to the central limit theorem which ensures that sampling distribution of a partial slope coefficient estimator will be normally distributed despite the non normal distribution of error term in the population (Hanushek and Jackson 1977:68; Kmenta 1986). Bohrnstedt and Carter (1971) also show the robustness of regression analysis against violation of normality and that significance tests can be done in large samples even when this assumption cannot be justified substantively. Even Jobson (1991: 61) states that normality assumption simply requires a sufficiently close normal distribution because real data are discrete and bounded, and therefore, cannot be normally distributed.

Dealing with Non normality

If there is non-normality normal distribution can be obtained by transforming the scale of measurement employed (That is, by removing skew-ness and kurtosis by the following methods discussed by Jobson 1991; Hinkley 1975; John and Draper 1980). Use any of the following transformation methods to remove skew-ness: (a) Use Box-Cox λ method to transform the scale. (b) Approximating.λ. This is a trial and error approach to the determination of the maximum likelihood estimator of λ involves determination of Lm (λ) for a range of values of λ. (c) Alternative Approximation. This is a comparison of the deviations for the transformed data, $(y_m - y (i))$ to $(y(n - i + 1)$ -ym). (d) Negative Observation. If the data set contains negative observations the use of Box-Cox transformation will not stretch or shrink the entire scale in one direction. Therefore, a preliminary transformation of the form $Y = (X + L)$, L a positive constant, is recommended to ensure that all the values are positive. Kurtosis can be removed in a symmetric distribution by using a modified power transformation.

SPECIFICATION ERROR

This assumption refers to the careful selection and specification of variables. That is, relevant variables should not be omitted and irrelevant ones should not be included in the model and the variables should be correctly ordered in the model (Kmenta 1971:392). According to Pedhazur (1982:225), specification is a situation in which the researcher shows a theoretical model that describes how the independent variables affect the dependent variable. The correct causal ordering of variables in a model is described as the most critical assumption that researchers must meet (Land 1969; Lewis- Beck 1980; Kmenta 1971). Heise (1969:52) specifically states that the causal laws governing the system are established sufficiently to specify the causal priorities among variables in a way that is un-debatable.

Rationale

The justification for this assumption is to make sure that our model is a true picture of reality.

Causes of Specification Error

Any causal model may be misspecified for one or more of the following reasons (Bagozzi 1980:76; Berry and Feldman1985; Kmenta 1986:442; Freund and Wilson 1998):

1. Relevant variables may be included in the model, but the functional form of the relationship may not be properly specified.

2. Error terms are incorrectly entered into regression equation.

3. A model may be estimated with the wrong independent variables. That is, important variables are omitted or irrelevant variables are included or both.

4. Relevant causal paths are omitted or irrelevant ones are included in the model.

5. Variables in the model are measured on nominal and ordinal levels rather than interval or ratio.

6. Failing to account for relationships that are not strictly linear.

7. Meassurement error is not modeled.

Testing for Misspecification Errors

Misspecification error can be detected by any of the following tests:

1. By plotting error term against X. There is misspecification error if the mean of error term increases as X increases (Bibby 1977; Rao and Miller 1971: Chapter 5; Draper and Smith 1966: Chapter 3; Jobson 1991).

2. The hypothesis that no relevant explanatory variables have been omitted from the regression equation

$$\text{Ho: } \beta_2 = 0$$
$$\text{H}_{1:} \ \beta2 \neq 0$$

can be tested by using RESET test (Regression Specification Error Test) (Ramsey 1969) or Rainbow Test (Utts 1982) to compare two estimates of the variance of the regression disturbance both of which are unbiased if the null hypothesis is true and both are biased when it is not. This bias will generally be larger for one than for the other.

3. Tests for linearity could be used as tests for non-omission of relevant variables (Kmenta1986: Section 11-3).

4. Use Lack of Fit Test. χ^2 test may be used to detect a biased estimate of the true error variance (Freund and Wilson, 1998).

5. The best way to detect misspecification error is by using a theory to point to the relevant variable that may be measured and added to the empirical analysis. Retain in the analysis variables that have theoretical significance and drop those that have no theoretical significance (Berry and Feldman 1985).

Effects of Specification Error

Violation of this assumption may lead to the following consequences: Omissions of an important variable will cause the regression path coefficients (parameters) to be incorrectly estimated and inclusion of an unimportant variable will bias only the estimates of parameter variance, reducing the sensitivity of tests of statistical significance of the parameter, but not affecting the parameter estimates themselves (Schumm et al.1980: 252; Kmenta 1986). Deegan (1972); Uslaner (1976); Bohrnstedt and Carter (1971); Freund and Wilson (1998) also conclude that if we hypothesized the wrong model, then our estimation of that model will yield meaningless estimates.

Dealing with Specification Error

Violation of this assumption can be justified due to the exploratory nature of the study as an attempt of summarizing present knowledge in order to guide future research (Heise 1969: 66). Sound theory should be used to determine the relevant variables to be included and irrelevant variables to be excluded in the model.

RECURSIVENESS

In recursiveness it is assumed that the direction of relationship between the variables in the path model is unidirectional. That is, no two variables in the model are reciprocally related with each affecting the other. This can be shown thus:

$$X \rightarrow Y \quad NOT \quad X \leftrightarrow Y$$

That is, if X causes Y, Y cannot affect X either directly or through a chain of other variables (Heise 1969; Pedhazur 1982; Duncan 1975; Asher 1976; Berry 1984). It is also assumed that all pairs of error terms in the model are uncorrelated.

According to Namboodiri et al. (1975: 444-448); Duncan (1975: Chapter 4); and Heise (1975) a model is recursive if the following conditions are met:

1. The model must be hierarchical. That is, all endogenous variables in the model can be arranged and labeled in a sequence $X_1, X_2 \ldots Xn$ such that for any Xi, and Xj where $i < j$, Xj cannot be viewed as the cause of Xi, therefore, βij must be equal to zero.

2. Two endogenous variables must not be reciprocally related with each a direct cause of the other.

3. Endogenous variables affecting an endogenous variable in a causal order must not have indirect causal linkages.

4. Each error term is uncorrelated with all exogenous variables, and all other error terms in the model.

Rationale

The reasoning for recursiveness is to assume that the underlying mathematical model consists of a set of recursive equations (Heise 1969:45) in order to know which variable has an effect on the other or the direction of influence.

Testing for Recursiveness

Assumption of non-recursiveness can be tested by any of these methods:
1. Examine the path model to see if all the exogenous variables in the model are arranged causally prior the dependent variables and also that all the exogenous are not causally ordered to each other (Duncan 1975:26).
2. Use Two-Stage Least Squares (2SLS) (Berry 1984; Johnston 1972; Kmenta 1971; Rao and Miller 1971).
3. Indirect Least Squares (ILS) can be used to detect violation of this assumption (Berry 1984).
4. Full- Information Techniques (Christ 1966)
5. Use multiple indicator models (Costner and Schoenberg 1973; Sullivan and Feldman 1979; Zeller and Carmines 1980).
6. Instrumental variable can also be used to test recursiveness.

Effects of Violation

When this assumption is violated the direction of influence in the model becomes ambiguous. It is also difficult to identify the direct and indirect effects, which means that both independent and dependent variables cause each other. If OLS regression is used to estimate the coefficients of the model, the resulting estimates will be biased and inconsistent and, thus, give inaccurate assessment of the nature of the magnitude of causal effects.

ERROR TERMS AND INDEPENDENT VARIABLES ARE UNCORRELATED

This assumption states that the error terms and the independent variables are not correlated (Bohrnstedt and Carter 1971; Asher 1976; Kelejian and Oates 1974; Duncan 1975; Gujarati 1978; Heise 1969). This assumption is expressed mathematically by Gujarati (1978:40) thus:

$$\text{Cov}(\mu_i, X_i) = E[\mu_i - E(\mu_i)][X_i - E(X_i)]$$
$$= 0$$

The tenability of this assumption has been questioned (Pedhazur 1982: 35-36) when applied to non-experimental research. In non-experimental research independent variable explains a relatively small proportion of variance of the dependent variable and the remaining portion of the variance is due to variables not included in the model. As a result, it is very questionable to assume that none of these variables is correlated to the independent variable.

Rationale

The rationale for this assumption is to be able to assess the individual effect of X and μ on Y (Gujarati 1978:40).

Sources of Error Terms correlating with Independent Variables

The following conditions can lead to error terms correlating with independent variables (Allison 1999:124; Bohrnstedt and Carter 1971):

1. When some independent variables are omitted in the model, error term will correlate with independent variable if any of the omitted variables is correlated with the measured X's.

2. Error terms may correlate with independent variables due to a reversed causation between Y(dependent variable) and X (independent variable). That is, if Y has a causal effect on any of the X's, then μ will indirectly affect X's.

3. Another condition for correlation between error terms and independent variables is due to measurement error in the independent variables. If independent variables are measured with error that error becomes part of error term, which in turn may relate to the independent variables.

Testing for Error Terms correlating with Independent Variables

This assumption can be tested by examining the plot of residuals against independent variables to see if the error terms are randomly plotted against the independent variables (Bibby 1977; Rao and Miller 1971: Chapter 5; Draper and Smith 1966: Chapter 3; Schumm et al.1980: 257).

Effects of Violation

If this assumption is violated the least squares parameter estimates will be biased or lead to estimates with undesirable properties (Lewis-Beck 1980; Asher 1976). When the independent variables are correlated with the disturbances gross errors in estimating β can arise (Bohrnstedt and Carter 1971:127). Violation may also make it impossible to assess the individual effect of X and μ on Y (Gujarati 1978: 40).

Dealing with Correlation Between Error Terms and Independent Variables

This problem can be solved through the following methods (Allison 1999; Hayduk 1988; Green 1997; Gujarati 1995): (a). Use randomization process in collecting data. (b). Include omitted variables in the regression equation if the problem is due to omission of relevant variable in the model. (c). Get multiple indicators of the variable if the problem is due to measurement error. (d). Use simultaneous equation methods if the problem is due to reverse causation between Y, dependent variables, and X, independent variables.

IDENTIFICATION

The last assumption to be considered is the identification assumption, which states that the path model should be identified. A model is identified when there is the same number of knowns (correlations, rs) and unknowns (path co-efficients, ps) (Heise1969; Pedhazur1982; Asher1976; Duncan 1975). There is an identification problem (or the model is not identified) when the number of knowns is not equal to the number of unknowns. An identification problem in general arises because the combined forces of the theory and data constraints are insufficient to determine unique estimates of the structural coefficients.

Sources of Identification Problem

According to Hayduk (1988); Duncan (1975); Long (1983a) identification problems can be due to any of the following sources:

1. There may be models with large numbers of coefficients relative to the number of input covariance. Avoiding the insertion of coefficients into a model merely because effects are possible can solve this.

2. It could be due to reciprocal effects and causal loops. Including variables thought to cause one or the other, but not both of the reciprocally related variables can solve this.

3. If the variance of a conceptual level variable is free and if all the λ's (lambda's) linking that concept to observable indicators are free, the λ's (lambda's) and the concepts variance are not identified. This can be solved by always fixing at least one λ (lambda's) for each concept.

4. Models may contain many similar concepts or many error co-variances. The problem can be solved by including a common cause within the model or by wording questions differently.

Rationale

The reasoning for this assumption is to be able to obtain numerical estimates of the structural coefficients from the estimated reduced-form coefficients (Gujarati 1978: 365) in order to guide the researcher in estimating the value of path coefficients or the unknown parameters in a model from available empirical data.

Testing for Identification

The following methods can be used to detect violation of the assumption (Hayduk 1988; Berry 1984; Duncan 1975; Chatterjee and Price 1977; Asher 1976; Wonnacott 1979: Chapter 18; Hanushek and Jackson 1977:254-264):

1. The model can be tested for identification violation by writing the equation for each covariance/variance as a function of the structural coefficients. The model is identified if a coefficient can be calculated by only one function of the covariance; not identified (under-identified) if there is no combination of covariance providing the value for a coefficient; and over-identified if there are many ways to calculate a particular coefficient. The entire model is identified if all the coefficients in the model are identified, but not identified if a single coefficient in the model is not identified.

2. The Linear Combination Perspective is another technique to detect violation of identification.

3. The Order Condition method can be used for testing identification violation. This is a simple counting technique in which each equation in a model is tested for identification separately.

4. The Rank Condition is another technique to detect identification violation.

5. Large standard errors of the coefficients may signify unidentified coefficients.

6. One or more coefficients may not be identified if the information matrix (containing the second-order partials of all the coefficients) has no inverse (i.e. is singular or has a zero determinant).

7. Wildly unreasonable estimates are another signal of identification problems, as do impossible estimates: negative error variance, negative variances, or standardized coefficients exceeding 1.00.

8. Correlations between coefficients estimates exceeding about ± .9 may signify identification problems.

Effects of Violation

Violation of this assumption can lead to the following effects:

1. If the model is under identified, it will be impossible to estimate the structural coefficients in the equation even if we know the population variances and covariance (Duncan 1975: 82).

2. It may be possible to estimate the coefficients of an under identified structural equation by the method of ordinary least squares, but the resulting estimates will be inconsistent.

3. Since the parameters of under identified equations cannot be consistently estimated, the hypothesis about their values cannot be refuted by sample observations. That is, the underlying theory is, from a scientific viewpoint, incomplete (Kmenta 1971: 550).

4. If the model is over identified, *i.e.*, the number of equations is greater than the number of unknowns, the unique estimation of all the parameters of our model will be impossible (Gujarati 1978:359).

Dealing with Identification Problem

The best way to solve the identification problem is to prevent it through the following ways (Bielby and Hauser 1977; Kessler and Greenberg 1981; Land and Felson 1978; Reilly 1981; Kim 1984; Hayduk 1988):

1. Emphasize theoretical constraints by including all suspected absences of effects (fixed zero coefficient), effects of specifiable magnitude (fixed non-zero coefficients), equality or proportionality constraints (equal or proportion effect, equal or proportional error variances), and variables known to influence only a few of the variables entwined in dense causal webs. Models should be initially built with the minimum necessary coefficients to which other coefficients may be added later.

2. Fix measurement error variances on the basis of known data collection procedures or published reliabilities.

3. Determine the time order in which the values of the relevant variables appear.

4. Look for studies that documented the size of any of the effects in the model and if the studies show that some variable influences another with a specific magnitude of effect, inserting this size of effect as a fixed coefficient may help identify the model.

5. If a particular pair coefficients (e g. a reciprocal causal relation) is problematic, we can estimate a series of models where first one and then the other of the problematic coefficients is fixed at each of a series of values covering a full range of reasonable values for that coefficient.

SUMMARY

In this chapter, you have learned about the assumptions underlying the use of path analysis. Each assumption is clearly stated and explained. The rationale or theory justifying the use of each assumption is discussed. Different ways of detecting whether an assumption is violated is discussed including using theoretical considerations, plotting the least squares residuals against the sample values of independent variable (X), or the fitted values of dependent variable (Y) or using statistical techniques. The effects of violations and how to deal with such violations or the justification for using the technique despite the violations of the assumption is also considered. In Chapter 5, you will learn about how to estimate a causal model.

REFERENCES

Aldrich, J. and F.Nelson.1984. *Linear Probability, Probit and Logit Models.* Beverly Hills, GA: Sage.

Allen, Michael Patrick. 1997. *Understanding Regression Analysis.* New York: Plenum Press.

Allison, Paul D. 1999. *Multiple Regression: A Primer*. Thousand Oaks, CA: Pine Forge Press.

Asher, Herbert B. 1976. *Causal Modeling*. Beverly Hills, CA: Sage Publications.

Bagozzi, Richard P. 1980. *Causal Models in Marketing.* New York: John Wiley & Sons.

Baker, Bela O., Curtis F. Hardyck, and Lewis Petrinovich. 1966. "Weak Measurements Vs. Strong Statistics: An Empirical Critique of S. S. Steven's Prescription on Statistics." *Educational and Psychological Measurement* 26 (Summer): 291-309.

Belsey, D. A. 1984. "Demeaning Conditioning Diagnostics Through Centering {With Discussion}." *The American Statistician* 38:73-77.

Berk, K. N. 1977. "Tollerance and Condition in Regression Computations." Journal of the American Statistical Association 72: 46–53.

Berry, William D. and Staley Feldman.1985. *Multiple Regression in Practice*. Newbury Park, California: Sage Publications.

Berry, William D. 1984. *Non-recursive Causal Models*. Beverly Hills, CA: Sage.

Bielby, William T. and Robert M. Hauser. 1977. " Structural Equation Models." *Annual Review of Sociology* 3:137-161.

Bibby, J. 1977. "The General Linear Model: A Cautionary Tale." Pp. 35-79 in *The Analysis of Survey Data.* Vol. 2, *Model Fitting*, edited by C. A. O'Muircheartaigh and Clive Payne. New York: Wiley.

Block, F. E. 1978. "Measurement Error and Statistical Significance of An Independent Variable." *The American Statistician* 32 (February): 26-27.

Bohrnstedt, George W. 1970. "Reliability and Validity Assessment in Attitude Measurement." Pp. 80-99 in *Attitude Measurement,* edited by G. F. Summer. Chicago: Rand McNally

Bohrnstedt, George W. and T. Michael Carter.1971. "Robustness in Regression Analysis." Pp. 118 -146 in *Sociological Methodology,* edited by H. L. Costner. San Francisco: Jossey Bass.

Boneau, C. H. 1960. "The Effects of Violations of Assumptions Underlying the t Test." *Psychological Bulletin* 57: 49-64.

Borgatta, Edgar F. 1968. "My Student, The Purist: A Lament." *Sociological Quarterly* 9: 29-34.

———. 1970. "Reply to Jacobson: A Dirty Handkerchief is Not What I Really Wanted." *Sociological Quarterly* 11: 270-271.

Boyle, R. P. 1970. "Path Analysis and Ordinal Data." *American Journal of Sociology* 75 (January): 461- 480.

Burke, C. J. 1953. "Aptitude Scales and Statistics." *Psychological Review* 60: 73-75.

Carmines, E.G. and R. A. Zeller.1979. *Reliability and Validity Assessment.* Beverly Hills, CA: Sage.

Champion, Dean J. 1970. *Basic Statistics for Social Research.* New York: Harper & Row Publishers.

Chatterjee, Samprit and Betram Price. 1977. *Regression Analysis by Example.* New York: John Wiley and Sons.

———. 1991. *Regression Analysis by Example.* New York: John Wiley and Sons.

Christ, C.F. 1966. *Econometric Models and Methods.* New York: John Wiley.

Cochran, W. C. 1947. "Some Consequences When the Assumptions for The Analysis of Variance Are Not Satisfied." *Biometrics* 3: 22-38.

———. 1968. "Errors of Measurement in Statistics." *Technometrics* 10: 637-666.

———. 1970. "Some Effects of Errors of Measurement on Multiple Correlation." *Journal of The American Statistical Association* 65 (March): 22-34.

Costner, Hubert L.1959. "Theory, Deduction and Rules of Correspondence." *American Journal of Sociology* 75: 245-263.

Costner, Hubert L. and Ronald Schoenberg. 1973. "Diagnosing Indicator ills in Multiple Indicator Models." Pp. 167-199 in Structural Equation Models in the Social Sciences, edited by A. S. Goldberger and Ottis D. Duncan. New York: Seminar Press.

Cronbach, L J. 1951. "Coefficient Alpha and The Internal Structure of Tests." *Psychometrika* 16: 297-334.

Dawes, R. M. and B. Corrigan. 1974. "Linear Models in Decision Making." *Psychological Bulletin* 81(Feb.): 95-106

Deegan, J. 1972. "The Effects of Multicollinearity and Specification Error on Models of Political Behavior." Ph.D. Dissertation, University of Michigan.

Draper, Norma R. and Harry Smith. 1966. *Applied Regression Analysis*. New York: Wiley.

Duncan, Otis Dudley. 1975. *Introduction to Structural Equation Models*. New York: Academic Press.

Engle, R.F.1982. "Autoregressive Conditional Heteroskedasticity with Estimates of the Variance of United Kingdom Inflations." *Econometrica* 50 {July}: 987-1007.

Fomby, T. B.,R. O. Hill, and S. R. Johnson.1984. *Advanced Econometric Methods*. New York: Springer-Verlag.

Freund, Rudolph J. and William J. Wilson. 1998. *Regression Analysis: Statistical Modeling of A Response Variable*. San Diego, CA: Academic Press.

Friedrich, C. 1982. "In Defence of Multiplicative terms in Multiple Regression Equations." *American Journal of Political Science* 26{November}: 797-833.

Fuller, W. A. 1996. *Introduction to Statistical Time Series*. New York: Wiley.

Glejser, H. 1969. "A New Test for Heteroskedasticity." *Journal of the American Statistical Association* 57:316-323.

Greene, William F. 1997. *Econometric Analysis*. Upper Saddle River, NJ: Prentice Hall.

Gujarati, Damoder.1978. *Basic Econometrics*. New York: McGraw Hill

———. 1995. *Basic Econometrics*. New York: McGraw Hill.

Habibagahi, H. and J.L. Pratschke.1972. "A Comparison of the Power of the Von Neuman Ratio, Durbin -Watson and Geary Tests." *Review of Economics and Statistics* (May): 179-185.

Hanushek, E. A. and J.E. Jackson.1977. *Statistical Methods for Social Scientists*. New York: Academic Press.

Hausman, J. A.1978. "Specification Tests in Econometrics." *Econometrica* 46 (November):1251-1271.

Hayduk, Leslie A.1988. *Structural Equation Modeling with LISREL Essentials and Advances.* Baltimore:The John Hopkins University Press.

Heise, David R. 1969. "Problems in Path Analysis and Causal Inferences." Pp. 38-73 in *Sociological Methodology*, edited by E. F. Borgatta and G. W. Bohrnstedt. San Francisco: Jossey Bass.

———. 1975. Causal Analysis. New York: John Wiley & Sons, Inc.

Hibbs, D. A. 1974. "Problems of Statistical Estimation and Causal Inferences in Time Series Regression Analysis." Pp. 252-308 in *Sociological Methodology*, edited by H. L. Costner. 1973-1974, San Francisco: Jossey-Bass.

Hinkley, D.V.1975. "On Power Transformations to Symmetry." *Biometrika* 62: 101-111.

Hoaglin, C.,F. Mosteller, and J.W.Turkey.1985. *Exploring Data, Tables, Trends and Shapes*. New York: John Wiley and sons Inc.

Hoerl, A. E. and R.W. Kennard. 1970. "Ridge Regression:Biased Estimation for Non-Orthogonal Problems." *Technometrics* 12 (February): 55-67.

Huber, P. J. 1981. Robust Statistics. New York: John Wiley.

Jacobson,P. E.. 1970. "Some Comments to Console Edgar F. Borgatta." *Sociological Quarterly* 11: 259-265.

Jobson, J.D.1991. *Applied Multivariate Data Analysis*. Volume 1. *Regression and Experimental Design*. New York: Springer-Verlag.

John, J.A. and N. R.Draper.1980. "An Alternative Family of Transformations." *Applied Statistics* 29:190-197.

Johnson, R.A. and D.W. Wichern.1982. *Applied Multivariate Statistical Analysis.* Englewood Cliffs, N.J: Prentice-Hall.

Johnston, J.1972. *Econometric Methods.* New York: McGraw Hill.

Judge, G.G.,W.E. Griffiths, R.C. Hill, H. Lutkepohl, and T.Lee.1985. *The Theory and Practice of Econometrics.* New York: John Wiley and Sons Inc.

Kelejian, Harry H. and Wallace E. Oates. 1974. *Introduction to Ecocmetrics.* New York: Harper and Row Publishers.

Kessler, Ronald C. and David F. Greenberg.1981. *Linear Panel Analysis: Models of Quantitative Change.* New York:Academic Press.

Kim, Jae-On. 1984. "An Approach to Sensitivity Analysis in Sociological Research." *American Sociological Review* 49:272-282

Klecka, W.R. 1979. *Discriminant Analysis.* Beverly Hills, CA: Sage.

Kmenta, Jan. 1971. *Elements of Econometrics.* New York: Macmillan.

———. 1986. *Elements of Econometrics.* New York: Macmillan Publishing Co.

Labovitz, S. 1967. "Some Observations on Measurements and Statistics." *Social Forces* 46 (Dec.):151-160.

———. 1970. "The Assignment of Numbers to Rank Order Categories." *American Sociological Review* 35: 515-524.

Lahiri, K. and D. Egy.1981. "Joint Estimation and Testing for Functional Form and Heteroskedasticity." *Journal of Econmetrics*15 (February):299-307.

Land, Kenneth C. 1969. "Principles of Path Analysis." Pp. 3-37 in *Sociological Methodology*, edited by E. F. Borgatta and G. W. Bohrnstedt. San Fracisco: Jossey Bass.

Land, Kenneth C., and Marcus Felson.1978. "Sensitivity Analysis of Arbitrarily Identified Simultaneous-Equation Models.' *Sociological Methods and Research* 6:283-307.

Lemieux, P.1978. "A note on the Detection of Multicollinearity." *American Journal of Political Science* 22 (February): 183-186.

Lewis-Beck, M. S. 1977. "Influence Equality and Organizational Innovation in a Third -World Nation: An Additive-Non-additive Model." *American Journal of Political Science* 21(February):1-11.

———. 1980. *Applied Regression: An Introduction.* Beverly Hills, CA: Sage.

Long, J. Scott. 1983. *Covariance Structure Models:An Introduction to LISREL.* Beverly Hills, CA: Sage.

———. 1983a. *Confirmatory Factor Analysis: A Preface to LISREL.* Beverly Hills, CA: Sage.

Lyons, M. 1971. "Techniques for Using Ordinal Measures in Regression and Path Analysis." Pp. 147-171 in *Sociological Methodology,* edited by H. Costner. San Francisco: Jossey Bass.

Lyons, M. and T. M. Carter. 1971. "Comments on Boyle's Path Analysis and Ordinal Data." *American Journal of Sociology* 76: 1112-1132.

McAdams, C. 1984. "The Errors in the Variables Problem in Political Science Data." Presented at the 1984 Meeting of the American Political Science Association, Washington DC.

McClendon, McKee J. 1994. *Multiple Regression and Causal Analysis*. Itasca, Illinois: F. E. Peacock Publishers, Inc.

Mclver, J. P. and E. G. Carmines.1981. *Unidimensional Scaling*. Beverly Hills, G.A: Sage.

Mendenhall, William M. and Terry Sincich. 1996. *A Second Course in Statistics: Regression Analysis*. Upper Saddle River, NJ: Prentice Hall.

Mertler, Craig A. and Rachel A. Vannatta. 2001. *Advanced and Multivariate Statistical Methods: Practical Application and Interpretation*. Los Angeles, CA: Pyrczak Publishing.

Mood, Alexander McFarlane. 1950. *Introduction to The Theory of Statistics*. New York: McGraw Hill.

Mosteller, F. and J. W. Turkey. 1977. *Data Analysis and Regression*. Reading, MA: Addison-Wesley.

Namboodiri, N. K., L. E. Carter, and H. M. Blalock. 1975. *Applied Multivariate Analysis and Experimental Designs*. New York: McGraw Hill.

Norvick, M. & G. Lewis. 1967. "Coefficient Alpha and The Reliability of Composite Measurements." *Psychometrica* 32: 1- 13.

Nunnaly, J. C. 1964. *Educational Measurement and Evaluation*. New York: McGraw Hill.

Ostle, B. & R. W. Mensing. 1975. *Statistics in Research*. Ames, IA: Iowa State University Press.

Ostrom, Charles W. 1978. *Time Series Analysis: Regression Techniques*. Beverly Hills CA: Sage Publication.

Pedhazur, Elazar J. 1982. *Multiple Regression in Behavioral Research: Explanation and Prediction*. New York: Holt, Rinehart & Winston.

Press, S. J. 1972. *Applied Multivariate Analysis*. New York: Holt, Rinehart, and Winston.

Ramsey, James B. 1969. "Tests for Specification Error in Classical Linear Least Square Regression Analysis." *Journal of The Royal Statistical Society* Series B, 31:350-371.

Rao, Potluri, and Roger L. Miller.1971. *Applied Econometrics*. California: Wadsworth Publishing Co.

Reilly, Thomas W. 1981. "Social Class Background and Women's Socialization into Parenthood." Ph. D. Dissertation, Department of Sociology, John Hopkins University, Baltimore, MD.

Sargan, J. D. 1958. "The Estimation of Economic Relationships Using Instrumental Variables." *Econometrica* 26(July): 393-415.

Schumm, Walter R., William T. Southerly, and Charles R. Figley. 1980. "Stumbling Block Or Stepping Stone: Path Analysis in Family Studies." *Journal of Marriage and The Family* (May): 251- 262.

Spitzer, J. J. 1984. "Variance Estimates in Models with Box-Cox Transformation Implications for Estimation and Hypothesis Testing." *Review of Economics and Statistics* 66 (November): 645-652.

Stanley, J. C. 1971. "Reliability." Pp.356-442 in *Educational Measurement*, edited by R. L. Thorndike. Washington, DC: American Council on Education.

Stevens, S, S. 1959. "Measurement." Pp.18-36 in *Measurement: Definition and Theories,* edited by C. W. Churchman. New York: Wiley.

Sullivan, J. L. and S. Feldman.1979. *Multiple Indicators: An Introduction.* Beverly Hills, CA: Sage.

Theil, H. and A. L. Nagar. 1961. "Testing the Independence of Regression Disturbances." *Journal of the American Statistical Association* 56:793-806.

Uslaner, E. M. 1976. *Regression Analysis: Simultaneous Equation Estimation.* Beverly Hill, CA: Sage.

Utts, Jessica M. 1982. "The Rainbow Test for Lack of Fit in Regression." *Communications in Statistics, Theory and Methods* 11: 2801-2815.

White, H. 1980. "A Heteroskedasticity- Consistent Covariance Matrix Estimator and a Direct Test for Heteroskedasticity." *Ecomonetrica* 48 (May): 817- 838.

Wilson, T. P. 1971. "Critique of Ordinal Variables." Pp. 415-431 in *Causal Models in the Social Sciences*, edited by H. M. Blalock. Chicago: Aldine- Atherton.

Wolinsky, F. D., S. A. Gernkovich, and L. J. Crisler. 1976. "Wizardry and Deception: A Research Note on Ordinal and Interval Path Regression." *Cornell Journal of Social Relations* 11 (Fall): 139-151.

Wonnacott, Ronald J. and Thomas H. Wonnacott. 1972. *Introductory Statistics.* New York: John Wiley.

———. 1979. *Econometrics.* New York: John Wiley.

Zeller, Richard A., and Edward G. Carmines. 1980. Measurement in the Social Sciences: The Link Between Theory and Data. New York: Cambridge University Press.

Chapter Five

Causal Model Estimation

The specified model can be represented in two ways: as an equation or in diagrammatic form. When stated as an equation, the causal model is rendered algebraically as a set of linear equations (structural equations), and is typically stated in its standardized form in which the direct causal effects are represented by "P" coefficients (path coefficients) e.g. $Z_1 = P_{41}Z_1 + P_{42}Z_2 + P_{43}Z_3 + e_4$.

The causal model is also portrayed in a path diagram (Figure 5.1), which is a pictorial representation of the theoretical explanations of the cause and effect relationships among a set of variables. In path diagram the variable at the head of one or more arrows is a function of those variables at the tails of the arrows.

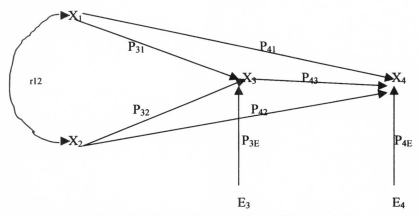

Figure 5.1. Original Path Diagram showing Path coefficient symbols

The system represented in the causal model (Figure 5.1) can be written thus:

$$X_3 = P_{31}X_1 + P_{32}X_2 + P_3EXE$$
$$X_4 = P_{41}X_1 + P_{42}X_2 + P_{43}X_3 + P_4EXE$$

Where P represents path coefficients, the first subscript identifies the dependent variable, the second the independent variable which indicates the direct effect on the dependent variable is measured by the path coefficient, X represents each variable, and E represents error terms. Here researchers admit the possibility that each of the Xi may be caused by all of the remaining variables (Blalock 1964: 53). Researchers using path analysis should be familiar with the two major problems in estimating path model: How to estimate the path coefficients, and how to decompose implied correlations into causal parameters (Bohrnstedt and Knoke 1982:420).

ESTIMATION OF PATH COEFFICIENTS

Path Coefficients are the numerical estimates of the causal relationships between two variables in a path analysis. Path coefficients are represented by Pij where the first subscript (i) represents the dependent variable, the second subscript (j) represents the independent variable. Path coefficients are important for the following reasons (Turkey 1954; Wright 1960; James etal.1982; Duncan 1975): (a) Path coefficients make algebraic and statistical manipulations simple, (b) they are based on correlation coefficients that are readily interpretable, (c) they are easy to interpret when all variables are standardized, and (d) in path analysis it is very simple to decompose the correlations into path coefficients.

Path coefficients are generally estimated by regressing each variable on the preceding variable. In other words, a separate regression calculation must be completed for each structural equation, each including only the direct causal effects of its associated endogenous (dependent) variable. Both path coefficients and multiple correlation coefficients are generally provided by standard computer regression programs available in the Statistical Product and Service Solutions (SPSS) computer software program for analysis of quantitative data (formerly the Statistical Package for the Social Sciences). See George and Mallery 2003: Chapter 16; Mertler and Vannatta 2001: Chapters 7&8; Kendrick 2000. For example in Figure 5.1 we regress X_3 on X_1 and X_2; and X_4 on X_1, X_2, and X_3. The correlations between independent variables (X_1, X_2) are simply taken as given and represented by a curve linking the pair of variables with arrow heads on both ends and does not represent any causal relationship or dependence between the variables. The correlation coefficients for X_1 and X_2 can be obtained by calculating the Pearson's r for X_1 and X_2.The coefficients for Es (error terms) are part of the equation indicating the numerical estimates of the variables not included in the model. Error terms can be calculated by taking the square root of $1-R^2$ for each endogenous variable

$$\sqrt{1 - R^2}$$

where R^2 is the square of the appropriate multiple correlation coefficient (MacDonald 1977; Bohrnstedt and Knoke 1982; Land 1969; McNemar 1962; Pedhazur 1982:585; Nunnaly 1978:129; Asher 1976:31).The path coefficient and Pearson's r can be generated by using a computer. See SPSS for appropriate programs (Kendrick 2000: Chapter 9; George and Mallery 2003: Chapters 10 & 16; Mertler and Vannatta 2001: Chapters 7 & 8; Morgan, Griego and Gloeckner 2001: Chapters 9&11).

DECOMPOSITION OF CORRELATION INTO CAUSAL PARAMETERS

Path correlation can be estimated through decomposition. Decomposition is the division of observed correlation coefficients between any two variables into four components: direct effect (D E) due to the path from X to Y (Figure 5.1, X_1 to X_4); indirect effect (I E) due to paths through intermediate variables (Figure 5.1, X_1 through X_3 to X_4); unanalyzed (U) due to correlated exogenous variables (Figure 5.1, X_1 to X_2); and spurious (S) due to third variable causes. Not all correlations are composed of all four parts. There are two methods of decomposing a correlation coefficient: the numerical or algebraic method, and the path tracing method. These methods will be explained with illustrations in the rest of this chapter from which researchers may choose to demonstrate causal relationships.

I. NUMERIC OR ALGEBRAIC METHOD

The numeric or algebraic method of estimating path equations is done by going through the following steps of normal equations (Bohrnstedt and Knoke 1982; Duncan 1966; Duncan et. al. 1972; Land 1969; Wright 1960a,

1960b; Duncan 1970b; Heise 1969; Kerlinger and Pedhazur 1973; Manuel 1981):

1. Multiply both sides of the equation by appropriate X

2. Sum both sides of this equation over sample observation. NOTE: P's may be written to the left of the summation signs (Σ) because they are constants.

3. Divide both sides of the equations by N where N is the number of cases in the sample.

4. Simplify the results by taking two assumptions into accounts:

a. A variable correlated by it self is 1.0 or unity.

For example:

$$\frac{\Sigma X_1 X_1}{N} = r_{11} = 1.0 \qquad \frac{\Sigma X_2 X_2}{N} = r_{22} = 1.0 \text{ etc.} \qquad \frac{\Sigma X_1 X_E}{N} = r_{1E}$$

Substitute this information into the linear (structural) equation. Example $r_{23} = P_{32} + P_{31} r_{12}$

b. Assumption of error terms.

The correlation between an independent variable and the residual (error term) in each equation is zero. That is, $\Sigma P_{1E} X_E = 0$

Residuals (error terms) are uncorrelated with other predetermined variables, that is $P_{3E} X_E = P_{4E} X_E = 0$.

The residuals of several equations are uncorrelated *inter se*, that is, $E_3 = E_4 = 0$ (Bohrnstedt and Knoke 1982; Duncan et al. 1972:26-27; Duncan 1975:25-29; Land 1969; Kerlinger and Pedhazur 1973:311).

5. Repeat steps 1-4 for each independent variable in the equation.

ILLUSTRATION

Let us illustrate the numerical or algebraic method for our model.

$$X_3 = P_{31} X_1 + P_{32} X_2 + P_{3E} X_E$$
$$X_4 = P_{41} X_1 + P_{42} X_2 + P_{43} X_3 + P_{4E} X_E$$

1. Both sides of the equations are multiplied by appropriate X (Independent Variable) X_1, here. $X_1 X_3 = P_{31} X_1 X_1 + P_{32} X_1 X_2 + P_{3E} X_1 X_E$

2. Summation of both sides of the equation are taken

$$\Sigma X_1 X_3 = P_{31} \Sigma X_1 X_1 + P_{32} \Sigma X_1 X_2 + P_{3E} \Sigma X_1 X_E$$

3. Divide both sides of the equation by N.

$$\frac{\Sigma X_1 X_3}{N} = P_{31} \frac{\Sigma X_1 X_1}{N} + P_{32} \frac{\Sigma X_1 X_2}{N} + P_{3E} \frac{\Sigma X_1 X_E}{N}$$

4. Then simplify the results by taking into account that a variable correlated by itself is 1.00 or unity:

$$\frac{\Sigma X_1 X_3}{N} = r_{13} \quad \frac{\Sigma X_1 X_1}{N} = r_{11} = 1.0 \quad \frac{\Sigma X_1 X_2}{N} = r_{12} \quad \frac{\Sigma X_1 X_E}{N} = r_{1E}$$

Then substitute this information into the equation above, which yields:

$$r_{13} = P_{31} r_{11} + P_{32} r_{12} + P_{3E} r_{1E}$$

Also note the assumptions of the error terms; hence, $P_{3E} r_{1E} = 0$.

5. Repeat steps 1-4 for each independent variable in the equation.

1. Multiply both sides of the equation by appropriate X

$$X_2 X_3 = P_{31} X_1 X_2 + P_{32} X_2 X_2 + P_{3E} X_2 X_E$$
$$X_1 X_4 = P_{41} X_1 X_1 + P_{42} X_1 X_2 + P_{43} X_1 X_3 + P_{4E} X_1 X_E$$
$$X_2 X_4 = P_{41} X_1 X_2 + P_{42} X_2 X_2 + P_{43} X_2 X_3 + P_{4E} X_2 X_E$$
$$X_3 X_4 = P_{41} X_1 X_3 + P_{42} X_2 X_3 + P_{43} X_3 X_3 + P_{4E} X_3 X_E$$

2. Summation of both sides of the equation are taken

$$\Sigma X_2 X_3 = P_{31} \Sigma X_1 X_2 + P_{32} \Sigma X_2 X_2 + P_{3E} \Sigma X_2 X_E$$
$$\Sigma X_1 X_4 = P_{41} \Sigma X_1 X_1 + P_{42} \Sigma X_1 X_2 + P_{43} \Sigma X_1 X_3 + P_{4E} \Sigma X_1 X_E$$
$$\Sigma X_2 X_4 = P_{41} \Sigma X_1 X_2 + P_{42} \Sigma X_2 X_2 + P_{43} \Sigma X_2 X_3 + P_{4E} \Sigma X_2 X_E$$
$$\Sigma X_3 X_4 = P_{41} \Sigma X_1 X_3 + P_{42} \Sigma X_2 X_3 + P_{43} \Sigma X_3 X_3 + P_{4E} \Sigma X_3 X_E$$

3. Divide both sides of the equation by N

$$\frac{\Sigma X_2 X_3}{N} = P_{31} \frac{\Sigma X_1 X_2}{N} + P_{32} \frac{\Sigma X_2 X_2}{N} + P_{3E} \frac{\Sigma X_2 X_E}{N}$$

$$\frac{\Sigma X_1 X_4}{N} = P_{41} \frac{\Sigma X_1 X_1}{N} + P_{42} \frac{\Sigma X_1 X_2}{N} + P_{43} \frac{\Sigma X_1 X_3}{N} + P_{4E} \frac{\Sigma X_1 X_E}{N}$$

$$\frac{\Sigma X_2 X_4}{N} = P_{41} \frac{\Sigma X_1 X_2}{N} + P_{42} \frac{\Sigma X_2 X_2}{N} + P_{43} \frac{\Sigma X_2 X_3}{N} + P_{4E} \frac{\Sigma X_2 X_E}{N}$$

$$\frac{\Sigma X_3 X_4}{N} = P_{41}\frac{\Sigma X_1 X_3}{N} + P_{42}\frac{\Sigma X_2 X_3}{N} + P_{43}\frac{\Sigma X_3 X_3}{N} + P_{4E}\frac{\Sigma X_3 X_E}{N}$$

4. Simplify the results by taking into account that

$$\frac{\Sigma X_2 X_3}{N} = r_{23}, \frac{\Sigma X_1 X_2}{N} = r_{12}, \frac{\Sigma X_2 X_2}{N} = r_{22} = 1.0, \frac{\Sigma X_2 X_E}{N} = r_{2E}$$

$$\frac{\Sigma X_1 X_4}{N} = r_{14}, \frac{\Sigma X_1 X_1}{N} = r_{11} = 1.0, \frac{\Sigma X_1 X_2}{N} = r_{12}, \frac{\Sigma X_1 X_3}{N} = r_{13}, \frac{\Sigma X_1 X_E}{N} = r_{1E}$$

$$\frac{\Sigma X_2 X_4}{N} = r_{24}, \frac{\Sigma X_1 X_2}{N} = r_{12}, \frac{\Sigma X_2 X_2}{N} = r_{22} = 1.0, \frac{\Sigma X_2 X_3}{N} = r_{23}, \frac{\Sigma X_2 X_E}{N} = r_{2E}$$

$$\frac{\Sigma X_3 X_4}{N} = r_{34}, \frac{\Sigma X_1 X_3}{N} = r_{13}, \frac{\Sigma X_2 X_3}{N} = r_{23}, \frac{\Sigma X_3 X_3}{N} = r_{33} = 1.0, \frac{\Sigma X_3 X_E}{N} = r_{3E}$$

Then substitute this information into the equation above that yields:

$$r_{23} = P_{31}r_{12} + P_{32}r_{22} + P_{3E}r_{2E}$$
$$r_{14} = P_{41}r_{11} + P_{42}r_{12} + P_{43}r_{13} + P_{4E}r_{1E}$$
$$r_{24} = P_{41}r_{12} + P_{42}r_{22} + P_{43}r_{23} + P_{4E}r_{2E}$$
$$r_{34} = P_{41}r_{13} + P_{42}r_{23} + P_{43}r_{33} + P_{4E}r_{3E}$$

Also assume that

$$P_{3E}r_{2E} = 0, P_{4E}r_{1E} = 0, P_{4E}r_{2E} = 0, P_{4E}r_{3E} = 0$$
$$P_{3E}r_{1E} = P_{3E}r_{2E} = P_{4E}r_{1E} = P_{4E}r_{2E} = P_{4E}r_{3E} = 0$$
$$r_{1E} = r_{2E} = r_{3E} = 0$$

Based on the assumptions of the error terms stated above the residuals are canceled out and therefore not represented in the model. Hence the equation can be written:

$$r_{13} = P_{31} + P_{32}r_{12}$$
$$r_{23} = P_{31}r_{12} + P_{32}$$
$$r_{14} = P_{41} + P_{42}r_{12} + P_{43}r_{13}$$
$$r_{24} = P_{41}r_{12} + P_{42} + P_{43}r_{23}$$
$$r_{34} = P_{41}r_{13} + P_{42}r_{23} + P_{43}$$

After collecting our results as written above we can now substitute appropriate unknowns for the known in the equation. That is we change the correlation (r) to coefficient (p)

$$r_{13} = P_{31} + P_{32}r_{12}$$
$$r_{23} = P_{31}r_{12} + P_{32}$$
$$r_{14} = P_{41} + P_{42}r_{12} + P_{43}(P_{31} + P_{32}r_{12})$$
$$r_{24} = P_{41}r_{12} + P_{42} + P_{43}(P_{31}r_{12} + P_{32})$$
$$r_{34} = P_{41}(P_{31} + P_{32}r_{12}) + P_{42}(P_{31}r_{12} + P_{32}) + P_{43}$$

Now simplify these equations by multiplying where necessary which yields:

$$r_{13} = P_{31} + P_{32}r_{12}$$
$$r_{23} = P_{31}r_{12} + P_{32}$$
$$r_{14} = P_{41} + P_{42}r_{12} + P_{43}P_{31} + P_{43}P_{32}r_{12}$$
$$r_{24} = P_{41}r_{12} + P_{42} + P_{43}P_{31}r_{12} + P_{43}P_{32}$$
$$r_{34} = P_{41}P_{31} + P_{41}P_{32}r_{12} + P_{42}P_{31}r_{12} + P_{42}P_{32} + P_{43}$$

The correlation between the predetermined variables (X_1 and X_2) in this model is treated as given and unanalyzed and represented as r_{12}. This correlation between the predetermined variables only gives us the degree of association between them because they are not causally related.

This calculation completes the set of numeric estimates of decomposition of correlation coefficient. In the equation above, the right side of each of the final versions of the equation contains only path coefficients and correlations between the predetermined variables as stated in the general principle of correlation decomposition by Bohrnstedt and Knoke (1982:426).

II. PATH TRACING METHOD

Computation for the correlation coefficient can also be estimated by tracing the paths in the diagram through the following steps using Sewall Wright's (1921, 1934) multiplication rule as described by Bohrnstedt and Knoke (1982); Asher (1976); Duncan (1975); Stevens (1959); McClendon (1994); Tate (1992); Mertler and Vannatta (2001):

Step 1

Trace the arrow pointing on one dependent variable (*i*) back to the independent variables (*j*) to get the direct effect. Add all the compound paths found to this value.

Step 2

If there is an arrow from a third variable (q) to dependent variable (i), trace all the connections between dependent variable (i) and independent variable (j) which involve each third variable (q). Then multiply the values of the path coefficients for these compound paths, which may lead to two kinds of compound linkages:

    a. If the arrow comes directly or indirectly from variable q to both variables i and j, trace backward from i to q, then forward from q to j and multiply the coefficient values as you go. Treat each distinct compound pathway for a given q (third variable) separately.

    b. If the arrow comes from variable j to variable q which in turn sends the arrow to variable i (either in two steps or through other intervening variables), trace back from i through q to j and multiply the path values as you go along. If more than one distinct compound pathway exists, treat each separately.

Step 3

When tracing paths we must conform to Sewall Wright's (1921,1934) multiplication rules that state: a. No path may pass through the same variable more than once; b. No path may pass through a double headed curved arrow representing an unanalyzed correlation between exogenous variables (in our example, between variables X_1 and X_2) more than once in any single path; c. No path may go backward on (against the direction of) an arrow after the path has gone forward on a different arrow.

Step 4

Add together the direct and indirect path values to obtain the correlation between dependent and independent variables (Pij) implied by the causal model.

ILLUSTRATION

The path tracing method can be illustrated as follow:

X_1, X_3

Using rule 1, trace the arrow from dependent variable (i) to independent variable (j) to obtain the direct effect.

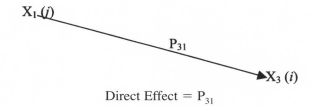

$$\text{Direct Effect} = P_{31}$$

Using rule 2, there is one "third" variable "q" (X_2) with direct path to X_3 (i). Trace backward from X_3 (i) to X_2 (q), then forward from X_2 (q) to X_1 (j).

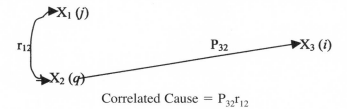

$$\text{Correlated Cause} = P_{32}r_{12}$$

Under rules 2a and 3b, we trace backward from X_3 to X_2 (P_{32}) and go through double headed curved arrow to reach X_1 (r_{12}). This compound path (correlated cause) is added to give $P_{32}r_{12}$. Applying rule 2b there is no indirect connections.

X_2, X_3

Using rule 1, trace the arrow from X_3 (i) back to X_2 (j) to obtain the direct effect

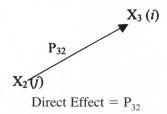

$$\text{Direct Effect} = P_{32}$$

Using rule 2, there is one "third" variable "q"(X_1) with direct path to X_3 (i). Trace backward from X_3 (i) to X_1 (q), then forward from X_1 (q) to X_2 (j).

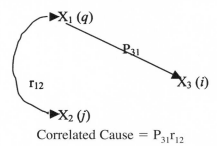

$$\text{Correlated Cause} = P_{31}r_{12}$$

Under rules 2a and 3b, we trace backward from X_3 to X_1 (P_{31}) and go through double headed arrow to reach X_2 (r_{12}). This compound path (correlated cause) is added to give $P_{31}r_{12}$. Applying rule 2b there is no indirect connections.

X_1, X_4.

Using rule 1, we trace the arrow from X_4 back to X_1 to obtain the direct effect

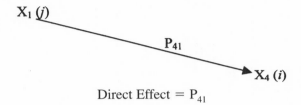

Direct Effect $= P_{41}$

There are two "third" variables X_2 (q_1) and X_3 (q_2) beside X_1 with direct path to X_4. We trace backward from X_4 to X_2 (P_{42}) and go through the double headed curved arrow to reach X_1 (r_{12}):

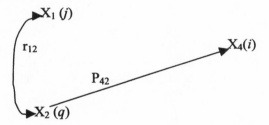

Such a compound path (correlated cause) gives: $P_{42}r_{12}$. We cannot violate rule 3a; hence, the second compound connection between X_4 and X_1 through X_2 is allowed. We trace from X_4 (i) back to X_3 (q_2) and from X_3 (q_2) back to X_2 (q_1) and go through the double- headed curved arrow to reach X_1 (j)

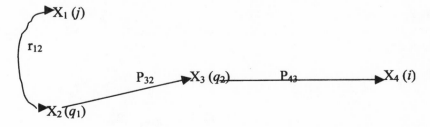

This correlated cause gives $P_{43}P_{32}r_{12}$. No other compound path via X_2 is possible. We now turn to the indirect connection involving X_3. One

involving X_2 has been noted, the only remaining compound path allowed by rule 2b is

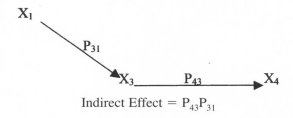

Indirect Effect $= P_{43}P_{31}$

X_2, X_4.

Using rule 1, we trace the arrow from X_4 back to X2 to obtain the direct effect

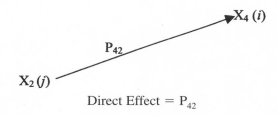

Direct Effect $= P_{42}$

There are two "third" variables X_1 (q_1) and X_3 (q_2) beside X_2 with direct path to X_4. We trace backward from X_4 to X_1 (P_{41}) and go through the double-headed curved arrow to reach X_2 (r_{12})

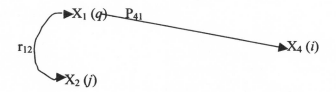

Such a compound path (correlated cause) gives: $P_{41}r_{12}$. We cannot violate rule 3a; hence, the second connection between X_4 and X_2 through X_1 is allowed

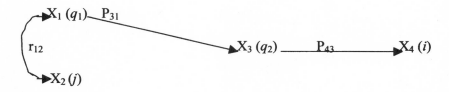

This correlated cause gives: $P_{43}P_{31}r_{12}$. No other compound path via X_1 is possible. We now turn to the indirect connection involving X_3. One involving X_1 has been noted, the only remaining compound path allowed by rule 2b is

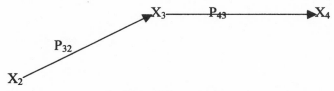

Indirect Effect: $P_{43}P_{32}$

X_3, X_4.

Using rule 1, we trace the arrow from X_4 back to X_3 to obtain the direct effect

$$X_3 \xrightarrow{\quad P_{43} \quad} X_4$$

Direct Effect $= P_{43}$

We trace backward from X_4 to X_1 (P_{41}) and forward to X_3 (P_{31})

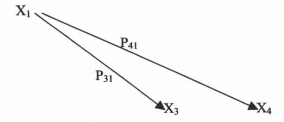

Such a compound path due to X_1 as a common cause yields: $P_{41}P_{31}$. Trace backward from X_4 to X_2 (P_{42}) and forward to X_3 (P_{32}). Such a compound path due to X_2 as a common cause yields: $P_{42}P_{32}$)

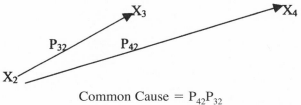

Common Cause $= P_{42}P_{32}$

We cannot violate rule 3a; hence, the second compound connection through the direct path from X_4 to X_1 and X_3 to X_2 is allowed.

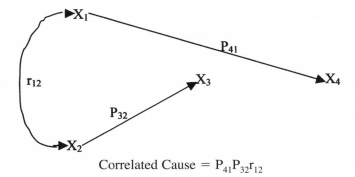

Correlated Cause $= P_{41}P_{32}r_{12}$

and through X_4 to X_2 and X_3 to X_1 is allowed.

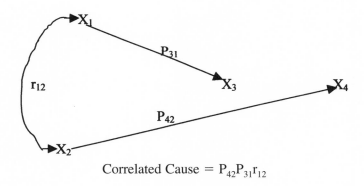

Correlated Cause $= P_{42}P_{31}r_{12}$

No other compound path via X_1 and X_2 is possible. Using 2b there is no remaining compound path to show indirect connections. By putting all paths together and reorder terms, we are able to arrive at the final decomposition of the correlations between the variables in the model.

X_1 and X_3
$$r_{13} = P_{31} + P_{32}r_{12}$$
X_2 and X_3
$$r_{23} = P_{32} + P_{31}r_{12}$$
X_1 and X_4
$$r_{14} = P_{41} + P_{42}r_{12} + P_{43}P_{32}r_{12} + P_{43}P_{31}$$
X_2 and X_4
$$r_{24} = P_{42} + P_{41}r_{12} + P_{43}P_{31}r_{12} + P_{43}P_{32}$$
X_3 and X_4
$$r_{34} = P_{43} + P_{41}P_{31} + P_{42}P_{32} + P_{41}P_{32}r_{12} + P_{42}P_{31}r_{12}$$

This is the same result obtained with algebraic method above. The entire correlation matrix from both methods of decomposition can be shown in terms of the path equation in table 5.1, and in calculation form in Table 5.2. Path decomposition is necessary because it helps in understanding how much of the correlations that we observed is due to direct effects, indirect effects, and third variables. It also helps us to better understand the theoretical processes as seen in the following tables:

Table 5.1. Path Decomposition for the Model shown in Figure 5.1

Reproduced Correlation	*Path Decomposition*		
Total Assoc	*Direct Effects*	*Indirect Effects*	*Non causal Effects*
r_{13} =	P_{31}	0	$P_{32}r_{12}$
r_{23} =	P_{32}	0	$P_{31}r_{12}$
r_{14} =	P_{41}	$P_{43}P_{31}$	$P_{42}r_{12} + P_{43}P_{32}r_{12}$
r_{24} =	P_{42}	$P_{43}P_{32}$	$P_{41}r_{12} + P_{43}P_{31}r_{12}$
r_{34} =	P_{43}	0	$P_{41}P_{31} + P_{41}P_{32}r_{12} + P_{42}P_{31}r_{12} + P_{42}P_{32}$

Table 5.2. Calculations of Reproduced Correlations for the Model shown in Fig. 5.1

Total Assoc	=	*Direct Effect*	+	*Indirect Effect*	+	*Non causal Effect*	=	*Total Effects*
r_{13}	=	P_{31}	+	0	+	$P_{32}r_{12}$		
		.37	+	0	+	(.26)(.43)	=	.4818
r_{23}	=	P_{32}	+	0	+	$P_{31}r_{12}$		
		.26	+	0	+	(.37)(.43)	=	.4191
r_{14}	=	P_{41}	+	$P_{43}P_{31}$	+	$P_{42}r_{12} + P_{43}P_{32}r_{12}$		
		.18	+	(.42)(.37)	+	(.16)(.43) +	=	.4512
						(.42)(.26)(.43)		
r_{24}	=	P_{42}	+	$P_{43}P_{32}$	+	$P_{41}r_{12} + P_{43}P_{31}r_{12}$		
		.16	+	(.42)(.26)	+	(.18)(.43) +	=	.4134
						(.42)(.37)(.43)		
r_{34}	=	P_{43}	+	0	+	$P_{41}P_{31} + P_{41}P_{32}r_{12} +$ $P_{42}P_{31}r_{12} + P_{42}P_{32}$		
		.42	+	0	+	(.18)(.37) +	=	.5738
						(.18)(.26)(.43) +		
						(.16)(.37)(.43) +		
						(.16)(.26)		

SUMMARY

This chapter has focused on the methods for the estimation of a given causal model. The Chapter started with discussion of two ways of representing causal model: as an equation or in diagram form. The problems facing researchers in estimating path model were identified: how to obtain path coefficients and how to decompose implied correlations into causal parameters. The procedures to obtain path coefficients using SPSS programs were discussed. Two methods of decomposing a correlation coefficient, the numeric method and path tracing method were considered. Each method was fully discussed with illustrations and the rules guiding them. The chapter ends with a table of decomposition of correlation coefficients into its component parts and another decomposition table showing the calculation for each component part. In the next chapter, practical research questions on path analysis are discussed.

REFERENCES

Asher, Herbert B.1976. *Causal Modeling*. Beverly Hills: Sage Publication.

Blalock, Hubert M. Jr. 1964. *Causal Inferences in Non-experimental Research*. Chapel Hill: The University of North Carolina Press.

Bohrnstedt, George W. and David Knoke. 1982. *Statistics for Social Data Analysis*. Illinois: P. E. Peacock Publisher, Inc.

Duncan, Otis D. 1966. "Path Analysis: Sociological Examples." *American Journal of Sociology* 72:1-16.

———.1970b. "Partials, Partitions, and Path." Pp.38-47 in *Sociological Methodology*, edited by E. Borgatta. San Francisco: Jossey Bass.

———.1975. *Introduction to Structural Equation Models*. New York: Academic Press.

Duncan, Otis D., David L. Featherman and Beverly Duncan.1972. *Socioeconomic Background and Achievement*. New York: Seminar Press.

George, Darren and Paul Mallery. 2003. *SPSS for Windows Step by Step: A Simple Guide and Reference*. Needham Heights, MA: Allyn & Bacon.

Heise, David R. 1969. "Problems in Path Analysis and Causal Inferences." Pp.38-73 in *Sociological Methodology*, edited by E. Borgatta, San Francisco: Jossey Bass.

James, Lawrence R., Stanley A. Mulaik, and Jeane M. Brett. 1982. *Causal Analysis: Assumptions, Models, and Data*. Beverly Hills: Sage Publications.

Kendrick,J. Richard. 2000. *Social Statistics: An Introduction Using SPSS for Windows*. Mountain View, CA: Mayfield Publishing Company.

Kerlinger, Fred N. and Elazur J. Pedhazur. 1973. *Multiple Regression in Behavioral Research*. New York: Holt, Rinehart and Winston, Inc.

Land, Kenneth C.1969. "Principles of Path Analysis." Pp.3-37 in *Sociological Methodology*, edited by E. F. Borgatta and G. W. Bohrnstedt. San Francisco Jossey Bass.

MacDonald, K. J.1977. "Path Analysis." Pp. 81-104 in *The Analysis of Survey Data*. Vol. 2, edited by G. A. O'Muircheartaigh and C. Payne. New York: Wiley and Sons.

Manuel, Ron C. 1981. *Advanced Statistics II Class Lecture*. Department of Sociology, Howard University, Washington, DC.

McClendon, McKee J. 1994. *Multiple Regression and Causal Analysis*. Itasca, Illinois: F. E. Peacock Publishers, Inc.

McNemar, Q.1962. *Psychological Statistics*. New York: Wiley.

Mertler, Craig A. and Rachel A. Vannatta. 2001. *Advanced and Multivariate Statistical Methods: Practical Application and Interpretation*. Los Angeles, CA: Pyrczak Publishing.

Morgan, George A., Orlando V. Griego and Gene W. Gloechner. 2001. *SPSS for Windows: An Introduction to Use and Interpretation in Research*. Mahwah, NJ: Lawrence Erlbaum Associates, Inc. Publishers.

Nunnaly, J. C. 1978. *Psychometric Theory*. New York: McGraw Hill.

Pedhazur, Elazur J. 1982. *Multiple Regressions in Behavioral Research*. New York: Holt, Rinehart and Winston.

Stevens, S. S.1959. "Measurement." Pp.18-36 in *Measurement: Definition and Theories*, edited by C. W. Churchman. New York: Wiley.

Tate, R. 1992. "General Linear Model Applications." Unpublished Manuscript, Florida State University

Turkey, J. W. 1954. "Causation, Regression and Path Analysis." Pp.35-66 in *Statistics and Mathematics in Biology*, edited by O. Kempthorne, T. A. Bancroft, J. W. Gowan and J. D. Lush. Ames, IA: Iowa State College Press.

Wright, Sewell.1921. "Correlation and Causation". *Journal of Agricultural Research* 20:557-585.

——. 1934. "The Method of Path Coefficients." *Annals of Mathematical Statistics* 5 (September):161-215.

——. 1960a. "Path Coefficients and Path Regressions: Alternative or Complementary Concepts?" *Biometrics*16: 189-202.

——. 1960b. "The Treatment of Reciprocal Interaction, with or without Lag in Path Analysis." *Biometrics*16: 423-445.

Chapter Six

Kinds of Research Questions on Path Model

The goal of research using path analysis is to illustrate the causal relationships between the variables. After model estimation, researchers should take into account some practical research questions in interpreting a path model as a means of illustrating such causal relationships. As a statistical tool, path analysis is very useful in answering a number of practical questions discussed in this chapter. The major research question for path analysis to answer is "Does our model fit the data?" (adequacy of the model). After assessing the adequacy of the model, path analysis can be used to address other questions about specific aspects of the model.

I. RESEARCH QUESTIONS ON THE FITNESS OF THE MODEL

Once the model has been specified properly and data were entered correctly, the fit of the data to the hypothesized model can be evaluated in the following questions: How adequate is the model? Are the theoretical assumptions postulated as explanatory relationships in the causal model substantiated by data?

There are many statistical techniques to evaluate the fit of a path model. However, in all the techniques, the researcher assumes that values of some parameters are based on theory; then the researcher estimates the correlation matrix based on assumed parameters; and finally the researcher then compares the observed correlation matrix to that which is based on theory to see whether the theory is accurate. That is, we can test the fit of the data to the model or theory by using Root Mean- Square Residual (RMR), X^2, or other measures under different indices discussed in this chapter. Unfortunately, there is no consensus as to which one is "best" because each test statistic has advantages and disadvantages, and there is no consensus regarding the effect of sample size and normality violations on different fit indices (Hu and Bentler 1995; Marsh, Balla and McDonald 1988). Therefore, it is important to examine many indices and not to rely solely on a single index when evaluating the fit of a model (Hoyle 1995b). Different methods of evaluating the adequacy of the model are classified into the following fit indices.

A. Absolute Fit Indices

The adequacy of the model can be evaluated by using the absolute fit-indices, which are designed to test whether the model fit is perfect in the population by comparing observed versus expected variances and co-variances given the relations among the variables specified by the model (Jaccard and Wan 1996). These fit indices are absolute in that they do not depend on a comparison with other models such as the independent or saturated models (CFI) or the observed data (GFI). The following test statistics under absolute indices can be used to evaluate the fit of the model:

1. Chi Square Test: This is a measure of fit rather than a test of statistics because it detects the degree of fit between the causal model and the data set to which it applies. It measures the difference between the sample covariance (correlation) matrix and the fitted covariance (correlation) matrix. If calculated X^2 exceeds a critical value of a predetermined probability level, one concludes that the model does not adequately represent the data that generate the pattern of relationships among the variables in the population. A small X^2 corresponds to good fit, and zero X^2 corresponds to a perfect fit (Anderson 1987, Joreskog 1993).

2. That the Chi Square assumption holds may not mean that the model fits the data. Thus we may have to consider other tests such as Goodness of Fit Indices (G F I) (Browne 1984; Bollen and Long 1993:6) through which we can measure the relative amount of variances and co-variances jointly accounted for by the model (Anderson 1987, Joreskog and Sorbom 1984). Examples of the goodness of fit measures are: The centrality index (CI) (McDonald 1989), the goodness of fit index (GFI.) and the adjusted goodness of fit Index (AGFI) proposed by Joreskog and Sorbom (1989). The GFI measures are to reduce the problem of dependence on sample size and to measure how much better the model fits compared with no model at all. Scores on all three indices can range from 0 to 1.0 with values closer to 1.0 being preferable. Values greater than .90 is an acceptable fit to many researchers, but there is no empirical support for this (Dilalla, 2000).

3. The Standardized Root Mean – Square Residual (SRMR) (Joreskog and Sorbom 1993a) which is the average discrepancy between the observed and the expected correlation across all parameter estimates, and the Root Mean Square Error of Approximation (RMSEA) (Steiger and Lind 1980) which adjusts for parsimony in the model are other absolute fit indices. A perfect fit will yield an RMR or RMSEA of zero; scores less than .08 are considered to be adequate and scores less than .05 are considered to be good (Jaccard and Wan 1996). The use of 90% of confidence interval to assess the error of approximation in the population was also suggested (Steiger 1990).

4. McDonald & Marsh (1990) proposed another absolute index, the relative non-centrality index (R N I), which does not depend on comparing models like the CFI or the GFI.

B. Comparative Fit Indices

Another method to evaluate the adequacy of the model is by comparing the indices. There are many methods in this category, but in each method the fit of a target model is compared to a baseline model.

1. The Comparative Fit Index (CFI) (Bentler 1990) compares the tested model to a null model having no paths that link the variables and thus the variables are independent of each other. Values in this index range from 0 to 1.0, and scores less than .90 indicate an unacceptable fit

2. The widely used comparative fit indices are The Normed Fit Index (NFI) (Bentler and Bonett 1980) and the Nonnormed Fit Index (NNFI) (Bentler and Bonett 1980) both of which are generalized versions of the Tucker and Lewis Index (TLI) (Tucker and Lewis 1973). Values less than .90 indicate an unacceptable model fit. TLI and the NNFI are very sensitive to the sample size and their values may not stay within the easily interpreted 0 to 1.0 ranges if the complete size is small. The NFI is more sensitive to violations of normality and to small sample size.

3. Comparison of several different models may be used to assess fitness confirmation of a model and the one that maximizes or minimizes some criterion tests is chosen. Sometimes the criterion chosen is the minimization of X^2 (Bollen and Long 1993; Biddle and Marlin 1987).

4. Sample Comparison. This can be done either by comparing a causal model developed for one population to another population that differs from the original by some variables. Data can be collected from a large sample in a particular study and split them into sub-samples, one for playing with and developing an appropriate causal model and the other for confirming that model with independent data (Biddle and Marlin1987).

5. The DELTA2 or Incremental fit Index (IFI) (Bollen 1989a) can be used to determine the improvement in fit between two models visa vis the baseline model and whether any meaningful information remains unexplained by the model. (See Anderson 1987 for more details). Fitting two models, one with correlated residuals and one without can test the hypothesis that the correlation between the residuals is zero. X^2 statistics for the two models can be compared using the IFI. If the decrease in X^2 that indicates an improvement in the models fit to the data is not significant, the model is acceptable (Anderson1987). It can range from 0 to 1.0, although values can exceed 1.0, which makes this more difficult to interpret than the GFI. Higher values indicate better model fit.

*Note Dilalla 2000:452 for suggested cutoff values for absolute fit indices and comparative fit indices.

C. Indices of Proportion of Variance Accounted

The fit of a model can be evaluated by the proportion of variance in the dependent variable explained by the independent variables included in the model. One method to evaluate the fit is done by computing the squared multiple correlation coefficient (R^2) for each structural equation (Specht 1975; Anderson 1987). The model is judged to fit the data when a goodly portion of the dependent variable variance is explained. A second method applies the GFI and the AGFI noted by Bentler (1983) and Tanaka and Huba (1989) are other techniques of evaluating the fitness of the model. These indices calculate a weighted proportion of variance in the sample covariance accounted for by the estimated population covariance matrix. Finally, a third method uses the proportion of variance in the explained variable r^2 that can be assigned to explanatory variable effects.

D. Degree of Parsimony Fit Indices

The Fit of a model can also be evaluated by the parsimony of the model. The principle of parsimony states that the best statistical model among all satisfactory models is that with the fewest parameters. That is, if the simplest model in terms of the number of variables or propositions can explain a phenomenon adequately then the simplest model should be selected. Because simple models are generally more replicable, model fit can be shown through its simplicity (Browne and Cudeck 1989; Cudeck and Browne 1983). One of the tests of parsimony fit to evaluate whether the model fits the data is The Parsimony Goodness-of-Fit Index (PGFI) (Mulaik et al. 1989), an adjusted form of the GFI. The closer to 1.0 the value of the fit index, the better the fit of the model. Other indices that can be used are the Akaike Information Criterion (AIC) and the Consistent Akaike Information Criterion (CAIC) proposed by Akaike (1987) and Bozdogan (1987); and the Expected Value of the Cross-Validation Index (ECVI) by Browne and Cudeck (1989). Small score values of AIC and CAIC indicate a fit parsimonious model.

E. Residual-Based Fit Indices.

Model fit can also be determined by the amount of variance in the model explained by variables not included in the model (residuals or error terms).

1. Small error terms indicate a good fit of the model to the data while large amount of error terms indicate that the model does not fit the data.

2. Residual based fit indices that can be used to test the adequacy of a model are the RMR, and the Standardized Root Mean-Square Residual (SRMR) by Hu and Bentler (1995). Good fitting models have small RMR and SRMR with values of .08 or less.

3. We can examine co-variance among disturbances to assess whether the model is confirmed. When all the co-variances are statistically insignificant, it is assumed that the model expresses all of the important variables affecting the data, and the model is confirmed.

4. The model may be said to fit the data if the correlations among the residuals of the measured variables in the model is close to zero. That is, the error terms are not correlated (Blau and Duncan 1967).

5. Another residual-based fit index to test adequacy of the model is to examine all standardized residuals collectively in two plots: a Stem-leaf plot and a Q-plot. A Stem-leaf plot with symmetrical residuals around zero and with most residuals in the middle and fewer in the tails indicate a good model. Excess residuals on the positive or negative side indicate that residuals may be systematically under or over estimated. In the Q-Plot, points falling approximately on a 45^0 line indicate a good model. Deviations from this pattern are indicative of specification errors in the model, non-normality in the variables, or non-linear relationship among the variables. Standardized residuals outliers in the Q-plot are indicative of a specification error in the model (Joreskog 1993).

F. Other Fit Indices

Other methods that can be used to evaluate the adequacy of a model are as follows. (a) Significance test for the disappearance of some selected partial correlation maybe used to indicate the fit of a model (Blalock 1964). (b) A test of significance of partial or multiple regression and correlation coefficients can be used. (c) Reconstruction of the zero order correlation matrices

from the estimated parameter can also be used. Such reproduced reconstructed correlations are compared with the observed correlations to test the
model fit. The model fits the data if the difference between the reconstructed
and the observed correlations is not more than a .05 difference (Duncan 1966;
Estep et al. 1977). (d) The significance or size of coefficients is another
method to evaluate adequacy of the model. (e) Examining its predictions
within the data set can also be used to assess a model. The models are confirmed when the relations they predict are mirrored by the statistically significant path diagram, or when the coefficients of these paths are larger than
some arbitrary standard.

Once the adequacy of the model had been established other research questions should focus on the following specific aspects of the model.

II. RESEARCH QUESTIONS ON INDEPENDENT VARIABLES

Many research questions on path model may focus on different aspects of the
independent variables in the model.

A. Importance of independent variables

What is the relative importance of an/the independent variable on the dependent variable?

What is the importance of the independent variable as a direct effect relative to other direct effects on a specified dependent variable?

What is the importance of the independent variable as a direct effect relative to its indirect effect?

What is the importance of its indirect effect relative to other ways it indirectly affects the same dependent variable?

What is the path coefficient for a specific path?

Does the coefficient differ significantly from 0?

B. Adding more independent variables

Have we improved our predictions of the dependent variables by adding more
independent variables?

C. Degree of relationship

What is the degree of correlation between the predetermined variables?

These research questions on independent variables may be addressed by
the following tests.

1. **Test for removing paths.** Researchers may like to test whether there is no direct effect between variables. Such a test depends on whether we are talking about one path or several paths within one equation. It must be understood that setting structural parameters equal to zero must be based on theoretical grounds as part of the original structural model. Hypothetical path coefficients in Figure 7.1 are used for illustration purposes.

a. Testing for no direct effect between two variables. That is one coefficient within an equation is zero. For example, we may postulate that there is no direct effect between X_1 (father's education) and X_3 (children's education) as shown in Figure 6.1.

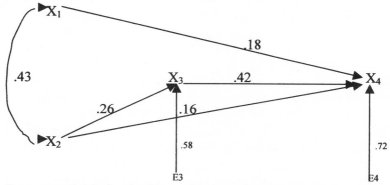

Figure 6.1. Original Path Diagram showing absence of a Path
$H_0: P_{31} = 0$
$H_1: P_{31} \neq 0$

When the path coefficient is hypothesized to equal zero, then one would predict that the estimated value should not differ significantly from zero. The statistics to test the significance of the parameter (β) is $t = b/sb$. That is, that path coefficient divided by its standard error.

$$t = b/sb$$

With $df = n - p - 1$ where n= number of cases and p = number of independent variables in the equation (Pedhazur 1982; MacDonald 1977:88; McPherson and Huang 1974; James, Mulaik, and Brett 1982).

If the calculated value of "t" is less than the (two tailed) critical value of "t" at a .05 level of significance, it is concluded that the path coefficient is not significantly different from zero and the Null hypothesis is confirmed. But if it is significantly different from zero the prediction is disconfirmed.

Z tests can also be used to test that a parameter is equal to zero (Anderson 1987: 53).

b. Testing for several coefficients within one equation.

If the hypothesis is that several coefficients in one equation are each zero. For example, in Figure 6.2, it is hypothesized that there are no direct effects between X_1 and X_3; and X_3 and X_4

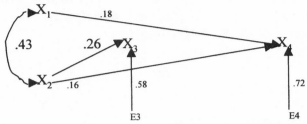

Figure 6.2.   Original Path Diagram Showing absences of two Paths
$H_0: P_{31} = 0$ and $P_{43} = 0$
$H_1: P_{31} \neq 0$ and $P_{43} \neq 0$

When the path coefficients are hypothesized to equal zero, then one would predict that the estimated values should not differ significantly from zero. Absence of several paths in the model can be tested for a hypothesis about q with Xr by using Hotelling's T^2 or F-test.

   (i) The Hotelling's T^2 test statistics can be used to test this hypothesis.

$$T^2q; n - k - 1$$

Where q is equal to the number of parameters to be tested in H_0 and k is the number of variables in the regression, with Xr as the dependent variable (McPherson and Huang 1974). If any of the parameter estimates of concern are different from zero at the a priori stated level of significance (.05) then the model is rejected by the data.

   (ii) Another test of statistics we can use is the F statistics

$$F = \frac{(R \, s \, s \, R - R \, S \, S \, u)/K}{R \, s \, s \, u/(n - p - 1)}$$

with the degree of freedom K for numerator and $n - p - 1$ for denominator Where RSS_R = the residual sum of squares from the restricted model (generated from full model), where Rssu = the residual sum of squares for the unrestricted model (generated from the model with omitted paths), k = the numbers of restrictions (variables omitted), n = the number of observations, and p = the number of independent variables in the unrestricted model (MacDonald 1977; Basmann 1960; Pedhazur 1982). If calculated F is greater than the critical value of F at a prior stated level of significance (.05), it is con-cluded that the difference is significant and hence the hypothesis is rejected.

2. **Test for comparing the magnitude of effects on the same variables.** The researcher may like to know which independent variable (X_1 or X_2) would produce a greater expected change in a particular or specified depen-dent variable (X_3) as shown in Figure 6.3. Hypothetical path coefficients in Figure 7.1 are used for illustration purposes.

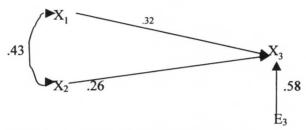

Figure 6.3. Original Path Diagram Comparing for Magnitude of Effects

To compare the magnitude of effects is not a problem if the two variables are of the same kind and on the same scale. Due to sampling error, we may de-termine whether the significance of difference between the direct effects re-flects a real difference in the population. This can be done by finding out whether a regression in which the effects of both variables were constrained to be equal would be significantly poorer than the regression obtained. F- test statistics can be used to test whether the constrained equation is significantly different from the unconstrained equation (MacDonald 1977:91-92).

$$F = \frac{(R\,s\,s\,R - R\,S\,S\,u)/K}{R\,S\,S\,u\,/(n - p - 1)}$$

See *F*- test statistics discussed above for explanation on equations.

3. **Testing for significant effects.** Another research question may focus on whether b differs significantly from any hypothesized value; that is, to test whether obtained b differs significantly from the population β. The standard-ized regression coefficient indicating the direct effect can be tested for statis-tical significance by using t test ratio.

$$t = b - \beta\,/sb$$

With df. $= N - k - 1$ where N = sample size, k = number of independent variables (Pedhazur 1982:29). If the observed value of t is greater than the critical value of t at a prior stated level of significance (.05 level), it is concluded that the hypothesis is confirmed.

4. **Comparison of relative importance of variables.** The researcher may be interested in finding out which of the variables X_1 or X_2 accounts for more of the variance in X_3 or which is the more important cause of X_3? Hypothetical path coefficients in Figure 7.1 are used for illustration purposes.

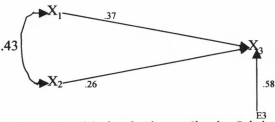

Figure 6.4.   Original Path Diagram Showing Relative Importance

The question of relative importance of a variable is very difficult to answer or unrealistic in a path model because it is difficult to apportion the variance between X_1 and X_2 unless they are completely independent i.e. they have zero inter-correlation (MacDonald 1977; Blalock 1961). Despite this concern the following techniques can be used to compare the relative importance of variables:

a. Compare the correlation coefficients (zero order correlation, r_S) of the independent variables. In Figure 6.4 we compare the correlation coefficients for X_1 and X_3 = .37 and X_2 and X_3 = .26. The variable with the greater correlation coefficient accounts for more of the variance in the dependent variable (Dawson and Robinson 1963; Hofferbert 1966; Biddle and Marlin 1987). This indicates that father's education (X_1) accounts for more of the variance in children's education (X_3).

b. Compare the partial correlation coefficients. For our example find the correlation between X_1 and X_3 by partialing out X_2 ($r_{13.2}$) and between X_2 and X_3 by partialing out X_1 ($r_{23.1}$). The variable with the greater partial correlation coefficient ($r_{13.2}$ or $r_{23.1}$) accounts for more of the variance in the dependent variable (X_3) (Dawson and Robinson 1963; Dye 1966; Shakansky and Hofferbert 1969).

c. Compare the multiple regression coefficients (βs). This is done by placing the variables of interest in a regression equation, calculate the standardized partial regression coefficients, and then compare their magnitude. Independent variable with the greater βs accounts for more variance in the dependent variable (Cnudde and McCrone 1969, Blalock 1967; Brooms and Halldorson 1973).

d. The best way to evaluate the relative importance of variables is to compare the effect coefficients because zero order correlation; partial correlation, and multiple regression coefficients are not the appropriate techniques in that generally they produce misleading judgments about the relative importance of variables (Lewis-Beck 1974, 1977; Blalock 1961b; Uslaner and Weber 1975; Tompkins 1975; Pedhazur 1982; Schoenberg 1972).

The effect coefficient, also called the total effects (TE), is calculated thus: The TE of a variable on another variable is equal to the sum of its direct effect (DE) plus its indirect effect (IE) (Duncan 1966; Land 1969:16; Lewis-Beck 1974, 1977; Lewis-Beck and Mohr 1976; Alwin and Hauser 1975; Duncan 1971; Finney 1972)

$$TE = DE + IE$$

The independent variable that has the greater effect coefficient (TE) accounts for more variance in the dependent variable or is the more important cause of the dependent variable. The effect coefficient technique when properly applied is more satisfactory than other methods in evaluating the relative importance of an independent variable on a particular dependent variable because it has generalized applicability and it is based on a more precise and comprehensive breakdown of relationship between two variables in the system into direct effect (DE), indirect effect (IE), spurious relation (S); and unanalyzed relation (μ) (Lewis-Beck1974, 1977; Wonnacott and Wonnacott 1970).

III. RESEARCH QUESTIONS ON DEPENDENT VARIABLES

Research questions on path model may also focus on the amount of variance explained in the dependent variables. Examples of such research questions are:

To what extent has the dependent variable been explained?
What is the relative magnitude or importance of each direct effect versus the corresponding indirect effect?
What is the relative magnitude or importance of each indirect effect for each independent variable?
What is the percentage or variance in the dependent variable due to variables not included in the model?
What is the relative magnitude of the direct effect/the indirect effect?
Which of the variables included in the analysis accounts for the most variance?

These questions can be answered through R^2- type statistics (Ullman 2001). Another method is to compute a total coefficient of determination for all the structural equations jointly. This statistics indicate the amount of variation in the dependent variable jointly accounted for by the model (Specht 1975; Anderson 1987).

IV. RESEARCH QUESTIONS ON INTERVENING VARIABLES

Questions on indirect effect of a variable focus on how one variable affects another variable in the model through an intermediary or mediating variable as follows:

To what extent has the variance of each intervening variable been explained by variables included/not included in the model?
What is the magnitude or importance of the direct effect of intervening variable relative to its indirect effects on a specified dependent variable?
What is the relative magnitude or importance of indirect effects of intervening variables on a specified dependent variable?
What is the importance of each specified direct effect of separate intervening variables relative to those indirect effects that include the variables of interest?

The following methods can be used for some of these research questions on intervening variables.

1. The researcher may be interested in comparing the magnitude of the direct and indirect effects. The question may be asked, "Is the difference between the direct and indirect effects significant?"

For example: Is there any difference between the effect of fathers education (X_1) on children's occupation (X_4), and father's education (X_1) on children's occupation (X_4) through children's education (X_3)? Hypothetical path coefficients in Figure 7.1 are used for illustration purposes.

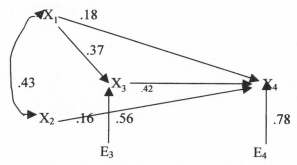

Figure 6.5   Original Path Diagram Showing Indirect Effects

When dealing with sample estimates of population parameters, it may be difficult to determine the sampling error for indirect paths generated from the regression output. The difference between direct and indirect effects may be significant due to the result of sampling error. Therefore, substantive interpretation may be more appropriate than statistical significance for such comparison. There is no fixed selection criterion for substantive meaningfulness but most researchers select .05 that is, the hypothesis will be significant if it is .05 or less. If the difference between direct and indirect effects is less than .05, the hypothesis is accepted because it is not substantively meaningful (Pedhazur 1982, Cohen1977).

2. Capturing of Paths. This is to test whether the intervening variables that are presumed to stand between and explain relations between independent and dependent variables, capture most of the paths that might otherwise tie independent to dependent variable. That is, to know whether the model includes proper intervening variables and the causal paths are correctly specified. The model is confirmed if there are few or no residual direct paths connecting independent and dependent variables in the analysis. The model does not include important intervening variables if one finds residuals with direct paths.

V. RESEARCH QUESTIONS
ON RELIABILITY OF VARIABLES

Reliability of variables is another important research question on path model. Researchers using path analysis must know the quality of measured variables they include in the model by making certain that the variables are reliable. Reliability of variables is very important in any statistical technique and path analysis can be used to test whether each of the variables included in the model is reliable. Reliable variables enhance an analysis and give a more meaningful solution. When variables are unreliable, the entire solution may reflect only measurement error.

Questions on reliability of variables can be: " How reliable are each of the measured variables in the model?" " Is the measure of Father's education reliable?" "How stable is the position of a given score in a distribution of scores when measured at different times or in different ways?"

Reliability of variables can be assessed by the following methods: Inter-Rater Reliability (a measure of agreement from one rater to other, rather than from time to time or even from test to test); Test-Retest Reliability (a measure of stability of an instrument over time. Are scores stable over time when the instrument is administered the second time?); Alternate Forms or Parallel

Forms (a measure of equivalence. How consistent it is from form to form?); and Internal Consistency (a measure of how consistently each item measures the same underlying construct. Are the items' responses consistent across construct?). The correlation for each of these methods will range between 0 and 1. One indicates "perfect" reliability; and 0.7 or higher indicates that the variable is sufficiently reliable to use (Stark and Roberts 2002; Kidder 1981; Carmine and Zeller 1979). Reliability of variables can also be assessed through Squared Multiple Correlation (SMC), where the measured variable is the dependent variable. Each SMC is interpreted as the reliability of the measured variable (Ullman 2001: 715).

VI. RESEARCH QUESTIONS ON TESTING THEORY

Path analysis is an important tool that helps us to determine whether or not a pattern of correlations for a set of observations is consistent with a specific theoretical formulation. Therefore, researchers may use path model to test the tenability of our theory. The following research questions on testing theory are important in path analysis:

Which theory produces an estimated population covariance matrix that is most consistent with the sample covariance matrix? Does adding (estimating) this covariance improve the fit of the model? Pedhazur (1973) and Ullman (2001) discussed the following methods of testing the tenability of our theory:

One method for testing the tenability of the theory is by comparing two models. The X^2 value for the larger model is subtracted the from X^2 value for the smaller nested model (models are subsets of each other) the difference, also X^2 is evaluated with degrees of freedom equal to the difference between the degrees of freedom of the two models. If the X^2 for the difference is significant, we conclude that the model fits the data. That is, the observed covariances among the measured variables arose because of the relationships between variables specified in the model. If the X^2 is not significant, we conclude that the model does not fit the data.

Another method of testing theory is to delete certain paths from the causal model. That is, certain path coefficients are set to equal zero. Before certain paths are deleted the correlation matrix (R) for all variables in the original model in which all the variables in the model are connected with paths are produced. After deleting certain paths, we also produce another correlation matrix (R) for the remaining variables connected with paths. Then we compare the correlation matrix (R) for the original model in which all variables are connected with paths with the correlation matrix (R) produced by the model with deleted paths. If the correlation matrix (R) for the model with deleted paths reproduces the original R matrix or a close approximation, it is concluded that the theory is tenable because the data are consistent with the model. But if there are large discrepancies between the original R and the reproduced one, it is concluded that the theory is not tenable because the model does not fit the data.

VII. RESEARCH QUESTIONS ON GROUP DIFFERENCES

Research questions on path model may be tailored to address differences between groups. Do groups differ in their covariance matrices, regression coefficients, or means? Does the model fit both groups in the experiment?

Using regression coefficients, variances and co-variances can test differences between groups. However, means, both latent and observed, can also be modeled (Sorbom 1974, 1982). The difference between the means is then estimated and evaluated with a Z test like any other parameters, where the estimated parameter is divided by standard error (For detailed discussion, see Bentler 1995; Byrne et al. 1989).

SUMMARY

This chapter has focused on research questions on different aspects of path model and how to address them. Research questions on adequacy of the model were addressed by using absolute fit indices, comparative fit indices, indices of proportion of variance accounted, degree of parsimony fit indices, and residual-based fit indices. Other questions about the following specific aspects of the model were also discussed, such as independent variables, dependent variables, intervening variables, testing theory, reliability of variables, and difference between groups with the appropriate methods to test them. Using path analysis to analyze social data also involves reading a path diagram, interpreting the results, reporting the findings, and using SPSS computer program, which are discussed in the next chapter.

REFERENCES

Akaike, H. 1987. "Factor Analysis and AIC." *Psychometrika*52: 317-332.
Alwin, Duane G. and Robert M. Hauser. 1975. "The Decomposition of Effects in Path Analysis." *American Sociological Review* 40(Feb.): 37-47.

Anderson, James G. 1987. "Structural Equation Models in the Social and Behavioral Sciences: Model Building." *Child Development* 58:49-64.

Basmann, R. L.1960. "On the Sample Distributions of Generalized Classical Linear Identifiability Test Statistics." *Journal of American Statistical Association* 55:650-659.

Bentler, P. M. and D. G. Bonnet. 1980. "Significance Tests and Goodness of Fit in the Analysis of Covariance Structure." *Psychological Bulletin* 88:588-606.

Bentler, P. M. 1983. "Some Contributions to Efficient Statistics in Structural Models: Specifications and Estimation of Moment Structures." *Psychometrika*48: 493- 517.

——. 1990. "Comparative Fit Indexes in Structural Models." *Psychological Bulletin* 107:238-246.

——. 1995. *EQS: Structural Equation Program Manual*. Encino, CA: Multivariate Software, Inc.

Biddle, Bruce J. and Marjorie M. Marlin.1987. "Causality, Confirmation, Credulity, and Structural Equation Modeling." *Child Development* 58:4-17.

Blalock, Hubert M. Jr. 1961b. "Evaluating the Relative Importance of Variables." *American Sociological Review* 26: 866-874.

——. 1964. *Causal Inferences in Non-experimental Research*. Chapel Hill: North Carolina Press.

——. 1967. "Causal Inferences, Closed Population, and Measures of Association." *American Political Science Review* 61(March): 130-136.

Blau, P. M. and Otis D. Duncan. 1967. *The American Occupational Structure*. New York: Wiley.

Bollen, Kenneth A. and J. Scott Long. 1993. "Introduction." Pp.1-10 in *Testing Structural Equation Models*, edited by Kenneth A. Bollen and J. Scott Long. California: Sage Publications.

Bollen, Kenneth A. 1986. "Sample Size and Bentler and Bonett's Non-normed Fit Index." *Psychometrika* 51: 375-377.

——. 1989a. "A New Incremental Fit Index for General Structural Equation Models." *Sociological Methods and Research* 17: 303-316.

Bozdogan, H. 1987. "Model Selection and Akaike's Information Criteria (AIC): The General Theory and Its Analytical Extensions." *Psychometrika* 52: 345-370.

Braungart, Richard G. 1971. "Family Status, Socialization, and Student Politics: A Multivariate Analysis." *American Journal of Sociology* 77, 108-129

Brooms, Bernard H. and James R. Halldorson. 1973. "The Politics of Redistribution: A Reformulation." *American Political Science Review* 67(September): 924-933.

Browne, M. W. 1984. "Asymptotically Distribution-Free Methods in the Analysis of Covariance Structure." *British Journal of Mathematics and Statistical Psychology* 37:62-83.

Browne, M. W. and Robert Cudeck. 1989. "Single Sample Cross-Validation Indices For Covariance Structures." *Multivariate Behavioral Research* 24: 445-455.

——. 1993. "Alternative Ways of Assessing Model Fit." Pp.136-163 in *Testing Structural Equation Models*, edited by Kenneth A. Bollen and J Scott Long. California: Sage Publication.

Byrne, B. M., R. J. Shavelson, and B. Muthen. 1989. "Testing for The Equivalence of Factor Covariance and Mean Structure: The Issue of Partial Measurement Invariance." *Psychological Bulletin* 105: 456-466.

Carmines, Edward G. and Richard A. Zeller. 1979. *Reliability and Validity Assessment*. Beverly Hills: CA: Sage.

Cnudde, Charles F. and Donald McCrone. 1969. "Party Competition and Welfare Policies in the American States." *American Political Science Review* 63(September): 858-866.

Cohen, J. 1977. *Statistical Power Analysis for Behavioral Sciences*. New York:Academic Press.

Cudeck, Robert and M. W. Browne. 1983. "Cross-Validation of Covariance Structures." *Multivariate Behavioral Research* 18: 147-167.

Dawson, Richard E. and James A. Robinson. 1963. "Inter-party Competition, Economic Variables, and Welfare Policies in the American States." *Journal of Politics* 25(May): 265-289.

Dilalla, Lisabeth F. 2000. "Structural Equation Modeling: Uses and Issues." Pp. 439-464 in *Handbook of Applied Multivariate Statistics and Mathematical Modeling*, edited by Howard E. A. Tinsley and Steven D. Brown. San Diego, CA: Academic Press.

Duncan, Otis D. 1966. "Path Analysis: Sociological Examples." *American Journal of Sociology* 72: 1-16.

———. 1971. "Path Analysis: Sociological Examples." Pp. 115-138 in *Causal Models in The Social Sciences*, edited by H. M. Blalock. Chicago: Aldine.

———. 1975. *Introduction to Structural Equation Models*. New York: Academic Press.

Dye, Thomas R. 1966. *Politics, Economics, and the Public Policy Outcome in the American States*. Chicago: Rand McNally.

Estep, R. E., M.R. Burt, and H. J. Milligram. 1977. "The Socialization of Sexual Identity." *Journal of Marriage and the Family* 39(February): 99-112.

Finney, John M. 1972. "Indirect Effects in Path Analysis." *Sociological Methods and Research* 2(November): 175-186.

Hofferbert, Richard I. 1966. "The Relation Between Public Policy and Some Structural and Experimental Variables in the American States." *American Political Science Review* 60(March): 73-82.

Hoyle, Rick H. 1995b. "The Structural Equation Modeling Approach: Basic Concepts and Fundamental Issues." Pp. 1-15 in *Structural Equation Modeling: Concepts, Issues, and Applications*, edited by Rick H. Hoyle. Thousand Oaks, CA: Sage Publications.

Hu, Li-Tze and Peter M. Bentler 1995. "Evaluating Model Fit." Pp.76-99 in *Structural Equation Modeling: Concepts, Issues, and Applications*, edited by Rick H. Hoyle. Thousand Oaks, CA: Sage Publications.

Jaccard, J. and C. K. Wan. 1996. *LISREL Approaches to Interaction Effects in Multiple Regression*. Thousand Oaks, CA: Sage.

James, Lawrence; Stanley A. Mulaik, and Jeanne M. Brett. 1982. *Causal Analysis: Assumptions, Models, and Data*. Beverly CA: Sage Publication.

Joreskog, Karl G. 1993. "Testing Structural Equation Models." Pp. 294-316 in *Testing Structural Equation Models*, edited by Kenneth A. Bollen and J. Scott Long. California: Sage Publication.

Joreskog, K. G. and D. Sorbom. 1984. *LISREL VI User's Guide. Mooresvile,* IN: Scientific Software.

———. 1989. *LISTREL 7: A Guide to the Program and Applications (2nd ed.).* Chicago: SPSS.

———. 1993a. *LISREL 8: Structural Equation Modeling with The SIMPLIS Command Language.* Hillsdale, NJ: Lawrence Erlbaum Associates Publishers.

Kidder, Louise H. 1981. *Zelltis, Wrightsman and Cook's Research Methods in Social Relations.* New York: Holt, Rinehart and Winston.

Land, Kenneth C. 1969. "Principles of Path Analysis." Pp. 3-73 in *Sociological Methodology*, edited by E. F. Borgatta. San Francisco: Jossey Bass.

Lewis-Beck, Michael S. 1974. "Determining the Importance of an Independent Variable: A Path Analytic Solution." *Social Science Research* Vol.3, Number 2 (June): 95-107.

———. 1977. "The Relative Importance of Socioeconomic and Political Variables for Public Policy." *The American Political Science Review* Vol.71: 559-566.

Lewis-Beck, Michael S. and Lawrence B. Mohr. 1976. "Evaluating Effects of Independent Variables." *Political Methodology* 3: 27-41.

MacDonald, K. I. 1977. "Path Analysis." Pp.81-104 in *The Analysis of Survey Data* Vol. 2, edited by G. A. O'Muircheartaigh and C. Payne. New York: Wiley and Sons.

McDonald, R. P. 1989. "An Index of Goodness- of- Fit Based on Non-centrality." *Journal of Classification* 6: 97-103.

McDonald, R. P. and H. W. Marsh. 1990. "Choosing A Multivariate Model: Non-centrality and Goodness-of-Fit." *Psychological Bulletin* 107: 247-255.

McPherson, J. Miller and Cliff J. Huang. 1974. "Hypothesis Testing in Path Models." *Social Science Research* 3:127-139.

McPherson, J. Miller. 1976. "Theory Trimming." *Social Science Research* 5:95-105.

Marsh, H. W., J. R. Balla and R. P McDonald. 1988. "Goodness-of-Fit Indexes in Confirmatory Factor Analysis: The Effect of Sample Size." *Psychological Bulletin* 103: 391-410.

Mulaik, S. A., L. R. James, J. VanAlstine, N. Bennett, S. Lind, and C. D. Stillwell. 1989. "An Evaluation of Goodness-of-Fit Indices For Structural Equation Models." *Psychological Bulletin* 105: 430-445.

Pedhazur, Elazar J. 1982. *Multiple Regression in Behavioral Research.* New York:Holt, Rinehart and Winton.

Schoenberg, R. 1972. "Strategies for Meaningful Comparison." Pp.1-35 in *Sociological Methodology*, edited by H.L. Costner. San Francisco: Jossey Bass.

Sharkansky, Ira and Richard I. Hofferbert. 1969."Dimensions of State Politics, Economics, and Public Policy." *American Political Science Review* Vol.63: 867-879.

Sorbom, D. 1974. "A General Method for Studying Differences in Factor Means and Factor Structure Between Groups." *British Journal of Mathematical and Statistical Psychology* 27: 229-239.

———. 1989. "Model Modification." *Psychometrika* 54:371-384.

Specht, David A. 1975. "On the Evaluation of Causal Models." *Social Science Research* 4:113-139.

Stark, Rodney and Lynne Roberts. 2002. *Contemporary Social Research Methods: A Text Using MicroCase*. Belmont, CA: Wadsworth/Thomson Learning.

Steiger, J. H. and J. C. Lind. 1980. "Statistically-Based Tests for The Number of Common Factors." Paper presented at The Annual Meeting of Psychometric Society. Iowa City, IL.

Tabachnick, Barbara G. and Linda S. Fidell. 2001. *Using Multivariate Statistics*. Needham Height,MA: Allyn & Bacon.

Tanaka, J. S. and G. J. Huba. 1989. "A General Coefficient of Determination for Covariance Structure Models Under Arbitrary GLS Estimation." *British Journal of Mathematical and Statistical Psychology* 42: 233-239.

Tompkins, Gary L. 1975. "A Causal Model of State Welfare Expenditures." *Journal of Politics* 37(August): 392-416.

Turker, L. R. and C. Lewis. 1973. "A Reliability Coefficient for Maximum Likelihood Factor Analysis." *Psychometrika* 38:1-10

Ullman, Jodie B. 2001. "Structural Equation Modeling." Pp. 653-771 in *Using Multivariate Statistics*, edited by Barbara G. Tabachnick and Linda S. Fidell. Needham Heights, MA: Allyn & Bacon.

Uslaner, Eric M. and Ronald E. Weber. 1975. "The Politics of Redistribution: Toward a Model of the Policy Making Process in the American States." *American Politics Quarterly* 3(April): 130-170.

Wonnacott, Ronald J. and Thomas H. Wonnacott. 1970. *Econometrics*. New York: Wiley.

Chapter Seven

Useful Information in Applying Path Analysis

Our knowledge of using path analysis is incomplete if nothing is said about some relevant information needed in applying the technique. In applying path analysis, it is important that users are knowledgeable in reading a path diagram, interpreting the results of a path analysis, reporting path analysis results, and in using the SPSS program in conducting path analysis.

READING A PATH DIAGRAM

After inserting the path coefficients (beta) from the computer printout into a path diagram, users should follow these basic principles in reading the path diagram. (How coefficients are generated is discussed under SPSS program section in this chapter). Our model (Figure 7.1) with hypothetical path coefficients will be used for illustration purposes.

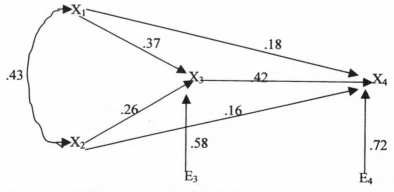

Figure 7.1. Original Diagram with Hypothetical Data
*P ≤ .05, ** P ≤ .01

Principle 1

Look at the different ways the independent variables affect the dependent variables. For example in Figure 7.1, we can see that father's education (X_1), and mother's education (X_2) affect children's education (X_3) directly. They also affect children's occupation (X_4) directly and indirectly through their influence on the intervening variable children's education (X_3).

Principle 2

Find out if the independent variables are correlated and the strength of their correlation. Figure 7.1 shows that the curved, two headed arrow between the two independent variables, father's education (X_1) and mother's education (X_2), $= r_{12} = .43$ indicates a correlation or relationship but not causal relationship between them. The strength of the correlation depends on the magnitude of the Pearson r which can be explained as follow: a weak relationship, $r = \pm 0.01 = \pm 0.30$; a moderate relationship, $r = \pm 0.31 - \pm 0.70$; a strong relationship, $r = \pm 0.71 - \pm 0.99$; a perfect relationship, $r = \pm 1.00$; and no relationship, $r = 0$.(Elifson et al. 1998:194). Therefore Figure 7.1 shows a moderate relationship ($r = .43$) between father's education and mother's education.

Principle 3

Read the path coefficients carefully. The numbers on the lines are the standardized regression coefficients from regressions used as path coefficients (β). For example the .42 on the line between X_3 (children's education) and X_4 (children's occupation) means that every 1.0 standard deviation increase in children's education leads to a .42 standard deviation increase in children's occupation. Negative path coefficients would indicate an inverse effect.

Principle 4

Find out the part of the dependent variables not explained by the independent variables, *i.e.*, part of the dependent variables explained by variables not included in the model. For example the number (.72) on the line coming from outside the system pointing to X_4 is the residual ("*e*","*u*"), a set of variables that also affects children's occupation but not included in the model. This is the part of the dependent variable X_4 (children's occupation) not explained by the independent variables. To find the percentage of children's occupation

(X_4) unexplained by the model, square the residual coefficient: .72x.72 =.5184. Which means 51.84% or about 52% of the total variance in children's occupation is unexplained by the model pictured in the diagram.

Principle 5

Find out how the following effects can be computed: Direct effect, Indirect effects, Total effects, Enhanced effects, Indirect effects of dependent variables on one another, Total effects of dependent variables on one another. (For detailed information on computation see Hayduck 1988; Bohrnstedt and Knoke 1982). Indirect effects can be computed by multiplying path coefficients for compound causal paths or chains of paths. For example, in Figure 7.1.the indirect effect of father's education (X_1) on children's occupation (X_4) is seen by multiplying the effect of father's education (X_1) on children's education (X_3) = .37 and by the effect of children's education (X_3) on children's occupation (X_4) = .42 which is .37 × .42 = .1554

Principle 6

Finally, look for indications of statistical significance. The asterisks (*; **; ***) indicate the * statistical significance of the path coefficients. Path coefficient with one asterisk (*) means that coefficient is significant at the .05 level, with two asterisks (**) is significant at the .01 level whereas the coefficient with three asterisks (***) is significant at the .001 level (For more details on reading a path diagram see: Vogt 1993; Allison 1999).

INTERPRETING PATH ANALYSIS RESULTS

After reading the path diagram, the next thing is to make sense out of the model by way of interpretation of what the path coefficients mean and how the variables affect one another. The statistical results generated by computer have to be interpreted because they seldom, if ever, speak for themselves. Statistical data in the raw simply furnish facts for someone to reason from and can be extremely useful when carefully collected and carefully interpreted.

i. Interpreting Path Diagram

In interpreting path analysis results, users may start with the path (beta) coefficients inserted into the path diagram (Figure 7.1) from the results reported in tables (7.1 to 7.5).

For illustration purposes, hypothetical computer outputs and coefficients are interpreted. Using the results shown in Figure 7.1, we will illustrate the interpretations usually made in path analysis as follows:

Direct Effect

Each direct effect in the path diagram should be interpreted as the amount of change in a dependent variable due to a unit change in independent variable if no effects are transmitted through intervening variables. For example the direct effect of X_1 on X_3 from this model is $P_{31} = .37$ (Figure 7.2). This means a unit change in father's education (X_1) leads to .37 unit change in children's education (X_3):

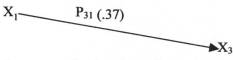

Figure 7.2.   Showing Direct Effect

Indirect Effects

Each indirect effect in the model should be calculated and interpreted as the magnitude of the predicted change in the dependent variables through intervening variables if the independent variable is changed 1 unit. Indirect effect can be calculated by multiplying path coefficients for compound causal paths. In Figure 7.3, the indirect effect of X_1 on X_4 shown thus:

Figure 7.3.   Showing Indirect Effect

is calculated thus: $(.37)(.42) = .1554$. This is interpreted as a unit change in father's education (X_1) leads to a .1554 unit change in children's occupation (X_4) through children's education (X_3).

Total Effect

Total effect on each dependent variable should be calculated and interpreted. This is the addition of the direct and indirect effects as shown in Figure 7.4:

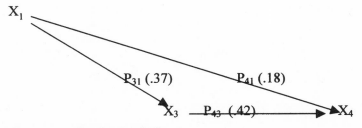

Figure 7.4. Showing Total Effect

Direct effect P_{41} (.18) and Indirect Effect $P_{31}P_{43}$ (.37 × .42) then Total effect = $P_{41} + P_{31}P_{43}$ (.18 + .37 × .42) = .3354. This is interpreted as .34 predicted unit change in children's occupation (X_4, the dependent variable) due to a unit change in father's education (X_1, the independent variable) if all the other variables in the model are left untouched except for changes originating in the hypothetical unit change in father's education (X_1).

Error Terms

Users may assess the completeness of each relevant subsystem by examining the path coefficients from the variables not included in the model. This is done by examining the error terms or residuals. In Figure 7.1 examination of unobserved variables (error term) reveals that 34% of the variation in children's education and 52% of the variation in children's occupation, respectively remain unexplained by the variables included in the model.

Unanalyzed Correlation

The double-arrowed curve between X_1 (father's education) and X_2 (mother's education) in Figure 7.1 represents an unanalyzed correlation generated by calculating Pearson's correlation. This is a non-causal relationship and is interpreted as the degree of association between two independent variables. In Figure 7.1 there is a moderate positive relationship (r_{12} = .43) between father's education (X_1) and mother's education (X_2).

There may be other path diagrams different from Figure 7.1 with some results of ambiguous causal relationships as discussed by Nie et al. 1975. Users of path analysis should be familiar with such results and how to interpret them.

Spurious Relationship

In a model in which the existing theory suggests a simple curve without arrows between the exogenous variables there is a spurious or non causal covariation between the variables as shown in Figure 7.5:

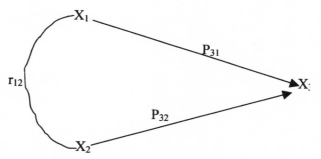

Figure 7.5.   Spurious Relationship between Exogenous Variables

The causal effect of X_1 or X_2 on X_3 is clearly defined. This can be interpreted as a unit change in X_1 would bring a P_{31} unit change in X_3, or a unit change in X_2 would bring a P_{32} unit change in X_3, on the assumption that changes in X_1 will not cause any change in X_2 and vice versa.

No Covariation

A model with no arrow or curve line between the exogenous variables as diagramed in Figure 7.6 can be interpreted as no co-variation between X_1 and X_2.

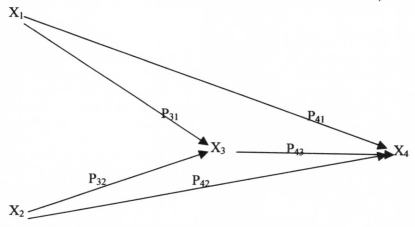

Figure 7.6.   Diagram of No Covariation Between Exogenous Variables

Bivariate Relationship

A model with a curve and an arrow line between the exogenous variables as diagramed in Figure 7.7 can be interpreted as a bivariate relationship that is partly causal and partly spurious:

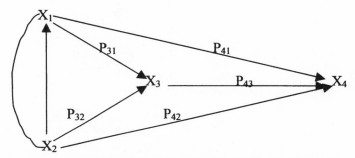

Figure 7.7. Partly Causal and Partly Spurious Relationship between X1 and X2

Interpretation of effects is limited to recursive models here. For detailed discussion on interpretation of other effects in non-recursive models, see Hayduk 1988: Chapter 8.

ii. Interpreting Tables

After interpreting the path (beta) coefficients transferred to the path diagram, other results reported in the tables should be interpreted. However, before interpreting the results in any statistical table, it is important that users read the table labels, legends, and the footnotes carefully (Allison 1999: 37). Once you have conducted all the regression analysis for the path model the computer will generate regression outputs including model summary, coefficients, correlations. The Model Summary Table 7.3 shows that the multiple correlation coefficients (R) is .72 and the adjusted R^2 is .64; meaning 64% of the variance in children's education can be predicted from father's education and mother's education. Note that the adjusted R^2 is lower than unadjusted R^2.

The correlation coefficients table in Table 7.3 is the most important table in interpreting path analysis results because it contains a constant, un-standardized coefficients (b), standardized coefficients (beta), t, significant level, and collinearity statistics. The un-standardized coefficients and the constant can be used to predict children's education score given their scores on father's education and mother's education. The standardized coefficient (β) with the respective level of significance should be noted within the path model.

Table 7.1. Outlier Determined by Mahalanobis Distance (Hypothetical Data)

		Extreme Values	*Case Number*	*Value*
MAH – 1	Highest	1	75	24.6151
		2	103	22.5106
		3	37	12.5641
		4	90	12.1541
		5	84	12.0566
	Lowest	1	36	.8956
		2	50	.9814
		3	55	1.1982
		4	40	1.2165
		5	93	1.3141

Un-standardized coefficient (b) is interpreted as the amount of unit change in the dependent variable due to a unit change in independent variable. The dependent variable changes by the number of units represented by the coefficient. For example (b = 3.521) is interpreted as with each additional year of father's education (independent variable), children's education goes up on the average by 3.521 and −1.711 is interpreted as with each additional year of mother's education, children's education goes down on the average by 1.711

The standardized coefficient (β or beta weight) tells us how many standard deviations the dependent variable changes with an increase of one standard deviation in the independent variable. For example, β = .372 can be interpreted as an increase of one standard deviation in father's year of schooling (independent variable) produces an increase of .372 standard deviation in children's year of schooling. And β = −.263 as an increase of one standard deviation in mother's year of schooling produces a decrease of .263 standard deviation in children's year of schooling. With β, we can compare the relative importance of the independent variables in the multivariate model, *i.e.*, which variable is more or less important in accounting for variation in the dependent variable?

Un-standardized coefficients (b's) for dummy variables e g. gender; race, marital status etc. (not reported here) can be interpreted as the average value of the dependent variable for all the people coded "1" on the dummy variable minus the average value of the dependent variable for others coded "0" on the dummy variable controlling for other variables in the model (Allison 1999). For example: gender (male = 1) = .114 means that males have years of education that average .114 points higher (or −.114 lower) than females; race (whites = 1) = .239 means that whites have years of education that is about .239 points higher (or lower if −.239) than nonwhites; and marital status

Table 7.2   Correlation Matrix for Model Variables (Hypothetical Data)

		Correlations			
		Father's Education	Mother's Education	Children's Education	Children's Occupation
Father's	Pearson Correlation	1.000	.433	−.821**	−.831**
Education	sig. (2 − tailed)		.000	.000	.001
	N	181	181	181	181
Mother's	Pearson Correlation	.433	1.000	−.513	.719
Education	sig. (2 − tailed)	.000		.000	.016
	N	181	181	181	181
Children's	Pearson Correlation	−.821	−.513	1.000	.720
Education	sig. (2 − tailed)	.000	.000		.001	.000
	N	181	181	181	181
Children's	Pearson Correlation	−.831	.719	.720	1.000
Occupation	sig. (2 − tailed)	.001	.016	.000	
	N	181	181	181	181

(married = 1) = .105 means that married people have years of education that is .105 points higher (or lower if − .105) than single people.

The "*t*" and *sig.* opposite each independent variable indicate whether that makes a significant addition to the prediction of all other variables; i.e., does the model add anything new? In Table 7.3 the path coefficients are significant.

Before interpreting the path coefficients, users should review the tolerance statistics for each exogenous variable included in each regression analysis in order to determine if multi-collinearity can be assumed. A low tolerance value (near 0) indicates extreme collinearity, that is, the given variable is almost a linear combination of other variables. A high value (near 1.00) indicates that the variable is relatively independent of other variables. If tolerance value is greater than .1, one may proceed with interpreting the path coefficients. For our examples, the tolerance statistics were all adequate.

Prior to conducting the regression analysis, a correlation matrix should be created (see Table7.2) because correlations will be needed later to test model fit.

Zero-order correlation or Pearson's r indicates the strength of relationship between a pair of variables. The Zero-order correlation table shows the correlation matrix, which is a summary of statistical relationship between all possible pairs of variables. The correlation can have values between + 1.0 and − 1.0, indicating the magnitude (or strength) of the relationship. A positive sign (+) means that there is a positive relationship between the variables, meaning that as one variable increases, the other variable also increases and vice versa. A negative sign (−) means that there is an inverse

Table: 7.3. **Regression Output For Children's Education (X_3) on Father's Education (X_1), and Mother's Education (X_2) (Hypothetical Data).**

Model Summary

Model	R	R^2	Adjusted R Square	Std. Error of the Estimate
1	.725ª*	.645*	.644**	3.50

a. Predictors: (Constant), Father's Education, Mother's Education
*Multiple Correlation
**Shows the amount of variance (64%) that can be predicted from the independent variables.

Coefficients

Model	Unstandardized Coefficients		Standardized Coefficients	t	sig.	Collinearity Statistics	
	B	Std. Error	Beta			Tollerance	VIF
1. (Constant)	15.611	1.212		37.731	.000		
Father's Educ.	3.521	.232	.372	12.035	.000	1.000	1.527
Mother's Educ.	−1.711	.099	−.263	−10.215*	.000	1.000	1.527

a. Dependent Variable: Children's Education
*Path Coefficients are significant

Table: 7.4. Regression Output For Children's Occupation (X_4) on Father's Education (X_1), Mother's Education (X_2), and Children's Education (X_3) (Hypothetical Data)

Model Summary

Model	R	R^2	Adjusted R Square	Std. Error of the Estimate
1	.768	.714	.726	2.32

a. Predictors: (Constant), Father's Educ., Mother's Educ., Children's Educ.

Coefficients

Model	Unstandardized Coefficients		Standardized Coefficients				Collinearity Statistics	
	B	Std. Error	Beta	t	sig.		Tolerance	VIF
1. (Constant)	64.180	1.552		45.083	.000			
Father's Educ	5.416	.057	.184	.760*	.326		1.000	1.010
Mother's Educ.	-6.624	.601	-.164	-6.913	.000		1.000	1.204
Children's Educ.	1.471	.212	.423	4.199	.000		1.000	1.645

a. Dependent Variable: Children's Occupation
*Path coefficient of children's occupation on father's education is not significant and should not be included.

Table: 7.5.   Observed and Reproduced Correlations For the
Model (Hypothetical Data)

	Observed Correlations			
	X1	*X2*	*X3*	*X4*
X₁	1.000			
X₂	.433	1.000		
X₃	.362	.125	1.000	
X₄	.485	.426	.251	1.000

	Reproduced Correlations			
	X1	*X2*	*X3*	*X4*
X₁	1.000			
X₂	.433	1.000		
X₃	.482	.419*	1.000	
X₄	.311	.353	.506*	1.000

*Difference between reproduced and observed correlation is greater than 0.05

relationship between the variables, meaning that increases in one are associated with decreases in the other and vice versa. "Non-causal relationship" is interpreted as the degree of strength of the relationship (not causal relationship) between two independent variables.

Variables must be evaluated to see whether the assumptions were violated. Interpreting output scatter plots can do this.

Outliers (Table 7.1) can be obtained by calculating Mohalanobis distance and conducting EXPLORE. Case number with value greater or exceeding the Chi-square criterion of 20.516 (d.f. = 5) should be eliminated from further analysis. Table 7.1 presents these results and indicates that case number 75 and case number 103 should be eliminated from further analysis since they exceed the Chi-square criterion of 20.516 (df. = 5).

The user must interpret model fit (Table 7.5) by comparing the reproduced correlations with the observed (empirical) correlations. If any reproduced correlation exhibit more than a .05 difference from the observed correlations, it means the model is not consistent with the data and should be revised. In Table 7.5, the difference between the reproduced and observed correlations is greater than .05. Therefore the model is not consistent with the data and should be revised.

Finally, users must be able to interpret the P- Value to decide whether or not the results support the null hypothesis. "P-value" (probability value) is to determine whether the coefficient is statistically significant or to identify the likelihood that a particular result may have occurred by chance. $P < .05$ is interpreted it is 5 in 100 probability that the result happens by chance, and a 95 probability that the result is reliable. Whenever the P-value is P < .05 or lower, the result is statistically significant, and supports the research hypothesis of a relationship between the variables, and rejects the null hypothesis that there is no relationship between the variables. P >.05 or lower means that the result does not support the research hypothesis stating a relationship between the variables but supports the null hypothesis of no relationship. That is, test results support the research hypothesis stating a relationship between variables whenever P < .05 or lower *but not* when P > .05 or lower. Therefore, users must attend carefully to the direction of the inequality symbol. That is, the smaller the P-value, the greater the likelihood that the findings are valid and reliable. According to George and Mallery (2003) results are considered statistically significant when P < = .05; marginally significant when it is between P < .05 and P > .10; and there is greater confidence that results are valid when P-value is below .05 (e.g. .01 .001, .0001 etc.). P-value with one asterisk (*) may indicate the coefficient is significant at the .05 level; with two asterisks (**) is significant at the .01 level; and with three asterisks (***) is significant at the .001 level etc. According to Stern and Kalof (1996), P < .05 and P < .01 may be stated in the text in any of the following ways: First, the results are statistically significant (or reliable) at the .01 level, second, alpha (α) was set at .05, and the result was significant, third, the null hypothesis was rejected with 95% confidence, and finally, the difference was statistically reliable at the .05 level.

Sometimes notation "n s" may replace a P-value. "n s" stands for "not significant", and that p-value is too large to reject the null hypothesis. For more details on interpretation of path analysis result, see Hayduk 1988: Chapter 8; Mertler and Vannatta 2001: Chapter 8; Morgan, Griego and Gloeckner 2001; Nie et al. 1975: 387-392.

PRESENTING PATH ANALYSIS RESULTS.

The goal of research using path analysis is incomplete if the findings are not communicated to the readers. In doing this, researchers must write out the results of the studies for readers to understand by including the following information in the analysis and report findings. This section provides a set of guidelines for presenting the results that allows readers clear model interpretation and evaluation (For details, see Raykov et al. 1991; Mertler and Vannatta 2001; Hoyle and Panter 1995).

Researchers should describe the conceptual and statistical models and report tables for readers to understand. In describing conceptually researchers are to present path diagrams that make explicit the relationship hypothesized among the variables under study. Each diagram should be clearly labeled and accompanied by written explanation and justification in the text for each proposed path or missing path. The written description at the bottom of each diagram should be in form of Figure XX. Presenting path diagrams will help to clarify the model being evaluated and also clearly illustrate the extent to which the theoretical model is confirmed (Alwin and Hauser 1975; Clark et al. 1978; Raykov et al. 1991; Hoyle and Panter 1995), and reporting tables will provide exact computations of effects. According to Allison (1999), the title of a Regression table must be written thus: Regression of Y (dependent variable) on X_1, X_2 etc (independent variables).

Information concerning the following items should be provided: (a) Researchers should provide tables of moment matrices (co-variances, cross-products, covariance/means, correlations) analyzed and some rationale for their choice of matrix to be analyzed. This should reflect the substantive concerns of the study and should be in accordance with the corresponding statistical theory (See Joreskog and Sorbom1988: Chapters 1 & 7;Cudeck 1989; McArdle 1988; Bentler 1989; Broomsma 1985). When space permits, researchers should report in a table, in an appendix or in the body of the manuscript the means and standard deviations of the entire set of variables used as input to path analysis. This will give the readers or other researchers the opportunity to carry out alternative data analyses from different theoretical perspectives, and suggest alternative models without repeating the expensive data collection process (Schumm et al.1980; American Psychological Association1996: 130; Hoyle and Panter 1995). Tables also assist readers in the interpretation of correlation coefficients as well as providing descriptive data about the sample, and necessary for archival purposes, if the study is included in meta-analysis.

(b) How missing data and outliers were treated should be explained so that it can be understood why the sample size used in the analysis is actually smaller than that reported under the sampling procedures. (Schumm et al. 1980; Lee 1977; Allison 1987; Bentler 1989: Chapter 9; Joreskog and Sorbom 1986, 1988)

(c) Information on the number of groups being analyzed should be provided. Such information should include the matrix analyzed for each group, means and standard deviations. Some rationale for each research hypothesis regarding group in-variances or differences should also be provided.

(d) Before presenting results, researchers should specify the method of parameter estimation for the models.

When presenting the results concerning the fit of model, a complete presentation of results necessitates disclosure of parameter estimates and statistics including the following measures: (a) chi square value, (b) degree of freedom,

(c) corresponding p-value, values of the following descriptive indexes of fit such as (d) goodness - of-fit index (GFI) and root-mean-square residual (for LISREL users: see Joreskog and Sorbom1988), (e) Bentler-Bornetts normed fit index (NFI), nonnormed fit index (NNFI), and comparative fit index (CFI) (for EQs users: see Bentler 1989, 1990); and (f) the parsimony ratio which provides information on the parsimony of model with regard to its number of free parameters (Bentler 1989, 1990; James, Mulaik and Brett 1982; Mulaik et al. 1989; McDonal and Marsh 1990).

Indexes of fit for different aspects of the model may also be reported when it is important to have an index measuring fit of the structural sub model alone (Mulaik et al 1989); when a simultaneous analysis of means and covariance structures is undertaken and the fit of the fitted means is estimated (Hertzog and Schaie 1988).

Researchers should provide a clear definition of each index, specifying the "critical value" of each index that will indicate acceptable fit, and justify in the manuscript the cut off value chosen (Hoyle and Panter 1995).

Researchers should provide information regarding poorly specified parts of the model. The goodness-of-fit, or lack of fit, of the model under consideration can be judged by an inspection of the obtained solution. Therefore, full information about parameter estimates should be explained and reported in the manuscript such as the following examples: measurement model factor loadings, specificities and covariance among factors, path coefficients, standard errors of the estimates, error variances-covariances, squared multiple correlations, and coefficient of determination (R^2) (Hoyle and Panter 1995). Researchers should make comments on the sign and size of the estimates and magnitude of the squared multiple correlations and coefficient of determination (Anderson and Gerbing 1988). Reporting R^2 presents important information so that the reader may have the opportunity, if he/she chooses to derive one set of coefficient from the other (Duncan 1975; Pedhazur 1982). Effect decomposition should be presented if the study focuses on it (Bentler 1989; Joreskog and Sorbom 1988).

The chi square values of each nested model along with their degree of freedom and corresponding p values; the difference in the chi square values, in the degree of freedom, and the associated probability value should be reported in tabular form (See Hertzog and Schaie 1986, 1988).

Researchers should describe how a modified or revised model was derived. Modification of models should be made on a theoretical basis (Anderson and Gerbing 1988) and should be reported as an alternative hypothesis to be tested and both the initial and the re-specified trimmed model should be reported (Thompson and Spanier 1978). Researchers should justify their choice for modifications of their models and report the values of the indices motivating these changes. Equivalent models should be reported either in a separate section of the Results section or as a component of interpretation of the Results in the Discussion for a clear understanding of what can be inferred from their results (Hoyle and Panter 1995).

Standardized (β) and un-standardized (b) path coefficients and the notation indicating their probability value (P-value) e.g., * P < .05, ** P < .01 etc. showing whether or not the coefficients are statistically significant should be reported. Significant coefficients should be indicated by the use of asterisks. Reporting both path coefficients will give investigators who are interested in comparing populations with different variance or doing longitudinal studies of a changing population with un-standardized coefficients needed (Heise 1975:127; Thompson and Spanier 1978; Biddle and Marlin 1987:5; American Psychological Association 1996:130; Hoyle and Panter 1995). So also reporting standard errors and "t" statistics in the regression table makes it possible for readers to calculate confidence intervals or exact p-values (Allison 1999). Estimates of reliability for measures (variables) should be reported (Katzer et al. 1991:104; Carmines and Zeller 1979:51).

In addition to the above information, a summary table of the causal effects showing the direct, indirect, and total effects for each endogenous variable should be presented.

SPSS PROGRAM FOR PATH ANALYSIS

Finally, researchers must know how to use the SPSS computer program in generating the value scores, diagrams etc. needed in path analysis. This can be done by using linear regression computer procedures through the following steps in the Statistical Product and Service Solutions (SPSS for windows) computer software program for the analysis of quantitative data.

Before using the SPSS program in path analysis, users must create and name a data file or edit an existing file. This is done through the following activities:

a. Prepare and collect survey questions.
b. Define and name variables.
c. Enter the data.
d. Check that data are entered correctly.
e. Save the data file in the diskette (3½ floppy A) or C Drive (Hard Drive). For details, see George and Mallery (2003: Chapter 3); and Kendrick (2000: Chapter 3). After completing the activities above users can use path analysis technique to analyze data through the following steps in SPSS Program:

Step 1

To enter SPSS Program

Click on START → Go to PROGRAM.
Click on SPSS 13.0 for Windows.

SPSS for Windows Screen will appear

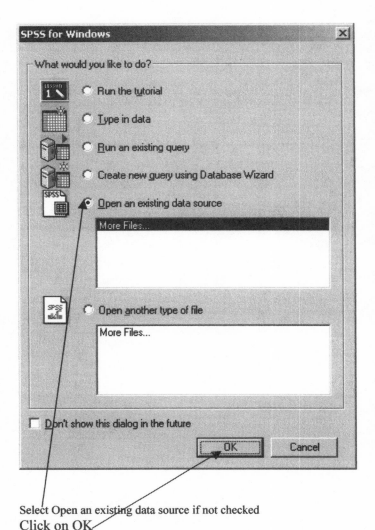

Select Open an existing data source if not checked
Click on OK

Step 2

Open File Screen will appear

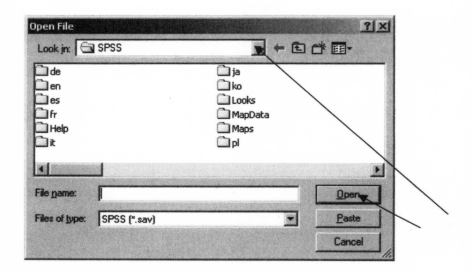

Insert 3½ Floppy (A) or CD

In Open File Screen click the push button in top line window

Select appropriate Saved Data File (Diskette 3½ Floppy A), CD or (C, Hard Drive)

Select Data desired

Click on OPEN

Step 3

SPSS Data Editor screen will appear

SPSS Data Editor Box screen with desired menu bars will appear. A series of options will appear when you Click on a command.

To open statistical options:

Click on ANALYZE → Go to REGRESSION
Click on LINEAR.

This will open the REGRESSION Dialogue Box shown below:

Step 4

Linear Regression Dialogue Box will appear

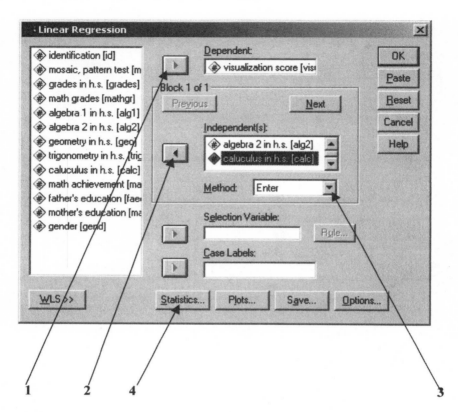

In the Linear Regression Dialogue Box, do the following activities:

i. Select and click the first Dependent Variable to be analyzed and move it to the Dependent Box by clicking the pushbutton. For our data, move children's education to the Dependent Box.

ii. Click each Independent Variable identified as having causal path to the specific Dependent Variable and move it to the Independent Box by clicking the pushbutton. For our data, click on father's education and mother's educations that were predicted would have causal effect on children's education.

iii. Under METHODS, select ENTER

iv. Click on STATISTICS (This will open a small Dialogue Box)

Step 5.

Linear Regression Statistics Screen will appear

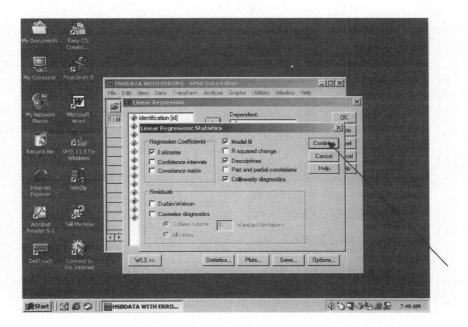

In the Linear Regression statistics Screen do the following activities:

   i. There are several statistical options to choose from

Select DESCRIPTIVES (This produces Means, Standard Deviations, or Correlation matrix)

Select ESTIMATES (Under Regression Coefficients)

This will produce B values, Beta and associated standard errors, t values, and significant values.

Select MODEL FIT and COLLINEARITY DIAGNOSTICS.

Model Fit will produce Multiple R, R^2, an ANOVA table, and associated F ratios and significant Values. Collinearity Diagnostics calculates Tolerance for each Independent Variable. This helps to explore whether collinearity exists among predictor and criterion variables.

ii. Click on CONTINUE, Linear Regression Screen will appear

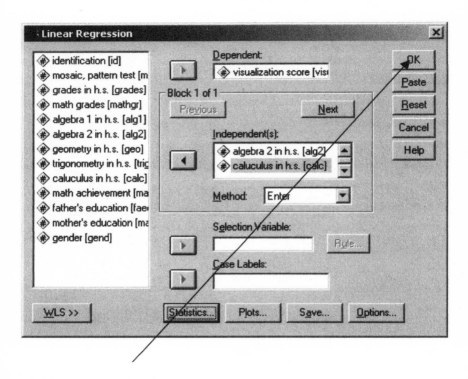

iii. Then click on OK.

Conduct this regression analysis procedure for each dependent variable in the model by going through steps 4 & 5.

Step 6.

Output SPSS View Screen will appear

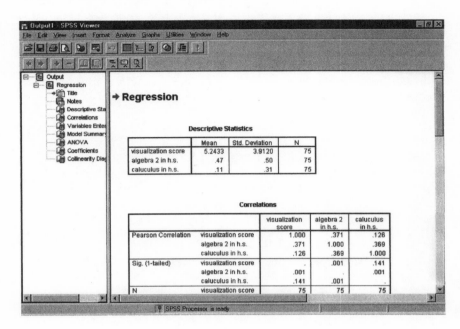

To print: Go to File
Click on Print
To EXIT: Click on File
Click on EXIT
NOTE: There will be small windows asking of you if you want to save or change anything. Simply click appropriate response

For our data, the following 2 analyses would be conducted:

Analysis	Dependent Variable	Independent Variable
1	Children's Education	Father's Education, Mother's Education.
2	Children's Occupation	Father's Education, Mother's Education, Children's Education.

For more details, on SPSS program, see George and Mallery (2003: Chapter 16); Mertler and Vannatta (2001: Chapters 7&8); Cronk (1999: Chapter 5); Sweet (1999: Chapter 6); Morgan, Griego and Gloeckner (2001: Chapter11).

SUMMARY

This chapter focused on the following important information needed by users/researchers in applying path analysis: How to read path diagram using some guiding principles was discussed. Interpretations of path analysis results were fully discussed using hypothetical data. Important information users should include in presenting or writing path analysis results were also discussed. Finally, the chapter ends with the steps to follow in using SPSS computer program in conducting path analysis through linear regression computer procedures.

REFERENCES

Allison, Paul D.1987. "Estimation of Linear Models with Incomplete Data." Pp.71-103 in *Sociological Methodology*, edited by C. Clogg. San Francisco: Jossey Bass.

———. 1999. *Multiple Regression: A Primer*. Thousand Oaks, CA: Pine Forge Press.

Alwin, D. F. and R. M. Hauser. 1975. "The Decomposition of Effects in Path Analysis." *American Sociological Review* 40(Feb.): 37-47.

American Psychological Association. 1996. *Publication Manual of the American Psychological Association*. Washington, DC.

Anderson, J. G. and D. W. Gerbing. 1988. "Structural Equation Modeling in Practice: A Review and Recommended two-step Approach." *Psychological Bulletin* 103:411-423.

Bentler, P. M. 1989. *EQS: A Structural Equation Program Manual*. Los Angeles: BMDP Statistical Software, Inc.

———. 1990. "Comparative Indexes in Structural Models." *Psychological Bulletin* 107:238-246.

Biddle, Bruce J., and Marjorie M. Marlin.1987. "Causality, Confirmation, Credulity, and Structural Equation Modeling." *Child Development* 58: 4-17.

Bohrnstedt, George W. and David Knoke. 1982. *Statistics for Social Data Analysis*. Illinois: P. E. Peacock Publisher, Inc.

Boomsma, A. 1985. "Non-convergence, Improper Solutions, and Starting Values in LISREL Maximum Likelihood Estimation." *Psychometrika* 50: 229-242.

Carmines, Edward G. and Richard A. Zeller.1979. *Reliability and Validity Assessment*. Beverly Hills: Sage Publications.

Clark, R. A., F. I. Nye, and V. Gecas. 1978. "Work Involvement and Marital Rule Performance." *Journal of Marriage and the Family* 40(February): 9-21.

Cronk, Brian C. 1999. *How to Use SPSS: A Step by Step Guide to Analysis and Interpretation*. Los Angeles, CA: Pyrczak Publishing.

Cudeck, R. 1989. "Analysis of Correlation Matrices Using Covariance Structure Models." *Psychological Bulletin* 105:317-327.

Duncan,Otis D. 1975. *Introduction to Structural Equation Models*. New York: Academic Press.

Elifson, Kirk , Richard P. Runyon and Audrey Haber.1998. *Fundamentals of Social Statistics*. New York: McGraw Hill.

George, Darren and Paul Mallery. 2003. *SPSS for Windows Step by Step: A Simple Guide and Reference*. Needham Heights, MA: Allyn and Bacon.

Hayduk, Leslie A.1988. *Structural Equation Modeling with LISREL.* Baltimore, MD: The John Hopkins University Press.

Heise, D. R. 1975. *Causal Analysis*. New York: Wiley.

Hertzog, C. and K. W. Schaie.1986."Stability and Change in Adult Intelligence: 1. Analysis of Longitudinal Covariance Structures." *Psychology and Aging* 1:159-171.

———. 1988. "Stability and Change in Adult Iintelligence:2. Simultaneous Analysis of Longitudinal Means and Covariance Structures." *Psychology and Aging* 3:122-130.

Hoyle, Rick H. and Abigail T. Panter. 1995. "Writing About Structural Equation Models." Pp. 158-176 in *Structural Equation Modeling: Concepts, Issues, and Application* edited by Rick H. Hoyle. Thousand Oaks, CA: Sage Publications, Inc.

James, L. R., S. A. Mulaik, and J. M. Brett.1982. *Causal Analysis, Assumptions, Models, and Data*. Beverly Hills, CA:Sage Publications.

Joreskog, K. G. and D. Sorbom.1986. *PRELIS: A Preprocessor for LISREL*. Mooresville, IN: Scientific Software Inc.

———. 1988. *LISREL 7: A Guide to The Program and its Application*. Chicago: SPSS Inc.

Katzer, Jeffrey, Kenneth H. Cook, and Wayne W. Crough.1991. *Evaluating Information: A Guide for Users of Social Science Research*. New York: McGraw Hill.

Kendrick, J. Richard. 2000. *Social Statistics: An Introduction Using SPSS For Windows*. Mountain View, CA: Mayfield Publishing Company.

Lee, G. R.1977. "Age at Marriage and Marital Satisfaction: A Multivariate Analysis with Implications for Marital Stability." *Journal of Marriage and The Family* 39(August): 493-504.

McArdle, J. J.1988. "Dynamic but Structural Equation Modeling of Repeated Measures Data." Pp.561-614 in *Handbook of Multivariate Experimental Psychology*, edited by R. B. Carttell and J. R. Nesselroade. New York: Plenum Press.

McDonald, R. P. and H. W. Marsh. 1990. "Choosing a Multivariate Model: Non-Centrality and Goodness of Fit." *Psychological Bulletin* 107:247-255.

Mertler, Craig A. and Rachel A. Vannatta. 2001. *Advanced and Multivariate Statistical Methods: Practical Application and Interpretation*. Los Angeles, CA: Pyrczak Publishing.

Morgan, George A., Orlando V. Griego and Gene W. Gloeckner. 2001. *SPSS For Windows: An Introduction to Use and Interpretation in Research*. Mahwah, NJ: Lawrence Erlbaum Associates, Inc., Publishers.

Mulaik, S. A., L. R. James, J. Van Alstine, N. Bennett, S. Lind, and C. D. Stillwell. 1989. "Evaluation of Goodness of Fit Indexes for Structural Equation Model." *Psychological Bulletin* 105:430-445.

Nie, H. Norman, C. Hadlai Hull, Jean G. Jenkins, Karin Steinbrenner and Dale H. Bent. 1975. *Statistical Package for The Social Sciences*. New York: McGraw Hill.

Pedhazur, E. J. 1982. *Multiple Regression in Behavioral Research 2*nd *ed.* New York: Holt, Rinehart & Winston.

Raykov, Tenko, Adrian Tomer, and John R. Nesselroade.1991. "Reporting structural Equation Modeling Result in Psychology and Aging: Some Proposed Guide lines." *Psychology and Aging* Vol.6., No. 4: 499-503.

Schumm, Walter R., William T. Southerly, and Charles R. Figley.1980. "Stumbling Block or Stepping Stone: Path Analysis in Family Studies." *Journal of Marriage and the Family* (May):251-262.

Stern, Paul C. and Linda Kalof. 1996. *Evaluating Social Science Research.* New York: Oxford University Press.

Sweet, Stephen A. 1999. *Data Analysis with SPSS.* Needham Heights, MA: Allyn and Bacon.

Thompson, L., and G. B. Spanier.1978. "Influence of Parents, Peers, and Partners on the Contraceptive Use of College men and Women." *Journal of Marriage and the Family* 40(August): 481-492.

Vogt, W. Paul. 1993. *Dictionary of Statistics and Methodology.* Newbury Park, CA: Sage Publications.

Index

Author's Biographical Sketch

Moses E, Olobatuyi is currently a sociology professor at Morgan State University, Baltimore, Maryland. He received his Ph.D. in sociology from Howard University with emphases in social psychology, research methods, and statistics. He has been teaching courses in these areas of specialization for 18 years. He also served at Hampton University, Lincoln University, and Saint Augustine's College and has published several articles in scholarly journals